MATHS
IN ACTION

Mathematics in Action Group

Members of the Mathematics in Action Group associated with this book:
D. Brown, R. D. Howat, E. C. K. Mullan, K. Nisbet, A. G. Robertson

FURTHER
QUESTIONS

Thomas Nelson and Sons Ltd
Nelson House Mayfield Road
Walton-on-Thames Surrey
KT12 5PL UK

Cover photograph by Darryl Williams/Steelcase Strafor plc

© Mathematics in Action Group 1994

First published by Blackie and Son Ltd 1986
New edition published by Thomas Nelson and Sons Ltd 1994

I(T)P Thomas Nelson is an International
    Thomson Publishing Company

I(T)P is used under licence

ISBN 0-17-431423-X
NPN 9 8 7 6 5 4 3

Printed in China

CONTENTS

INTRODUCTION

These *Further Questions* are intended to supplement the course developed in the series **Maths in Action**. They consist of exercises of harder questions, closely related to the corresponding (and similarly numbered) exercises in Book 2, and based on the text in Book 2. The 'F' notation, for example Exercise 1F, enables easy cross-reference to be made between these exercises and the A, B and C exercises in Book 2, especially where both are being used in the classroom or for homework.

1 NUMBERS IN ACTION

EXERCISE 1F

1

Planet	Diameter (km)	Distance from sun
Earth	12 756	149.60 million km
Mars	6786	227.94 million km
Jupiter	142 984	778.33 million km

The three planets are in a straight line out from the sun. Calculate, and write in figures, the distance:
a between the Earth and: (i) Mars   (ii) Jupiter
b travelled on a journey from the Earth to the Sun and then to Mars
c in a return journey from Mars to the Sun.

2 Using the data in the table in question **1**, how many times, to the nearest whole number, is the diameter of:
a the Earth, compared to Mars
b Jupiter, compared to the Earth
c Jupiter, compared to Mars.

3 These instructions change speeds in km/h to metres per second (m/s):

a Check that 60 km/h = 17 m/s, to the nearest whole unit.
b Change to m/s: (i) 720 km/h   (ii) 100 km/h   (iii) 4 km/h.
c List instructions for changing m/s to km/h.
d Use **c** to change to km/h: (i) 20 m/s   (ii) 75 m/s   (iii) 8 m/s

4 a You have £75. How many:
   (i) dollars
   (ii) marks
   would you get for it?

£1 = $1.53
£1 = 2.41 marks

b 1 franc = 12 pence. How many francs would you be given for:
(i) 1 dollar   (ii) 1 mark, using the rates given in part **a**?

EXERCISE 2F

1 a Write down the heights of these mountains to the nearest:
(i) 1000 m   (ii) 100 m   (iii) 10 m
b What is the difference between their heights to the nearest:
(i) metre   (ii) 10 m   (iii) 100 m?

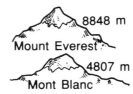

8848 m
Mount Everest

4807 m
Mont Blanc

2 Round the diameter of each of these planets to the nearest:
(i) 10 km   (ii) 100 km   (iii) 1000 km.

a Earth	12 756 km
b Mars	6786 km
c Jupiter	142 984 km

3

a UK	57.56 million
b Canada	30.2 million

These are estimated population figures for 2010.
In terms of 1000s what figure has each been rounded to?

4 These figures were quoted as the average daily sales of newspapers.
a Why are they not sensible?
b Round them off to an accurate number which you consider sensible and state your accuracy.

Star	916 196
Mail	1 663 896
Sun	3 879 630

5 China's estimated population for the year 2010 is 1382.46 million.
Round this to the nearest:
a hundred thousand   **b** million   **c** ten million   **d** hundred million

EXERCISE 3F

1 £1 = 2.4842 marks. Rounding your answers to 2 decimal places, convert to marks:
a £5   **b** £12   **c** £56   **d** £6.50   **e** £12.58

2 Calculate the volumes of these shapes, correct to 3 decimal places.

a

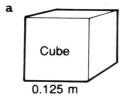

Cube

0.125 m

b

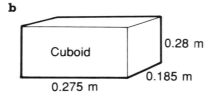

Cuboid

0.28 m

0.275 m

0.185 m

3 Between what lengths, to 2 decimal places, do these lengths lie?
a 6.5 cm   **b** 0.7 cm   **c** 13.1 cm   **d** 46 cm

4 Tony weighs 54 kg. Mark weighs 43 kg. Calculate the greatest and least values of:
a the sum   **b** the difference, of their weights.

5 An engineer measures a metal plate to be 4.6 cm by 8.2 cm. Calculate its greatest and least possible areas, correct to the nearest tenth of a cm².

6 The area of a square is 130.5 cm².
  a Estimate the length of one side.
  b Using only the ☒ key on your calculator and trial and improvement, calculate the length of one side, correct to 2 decimal places.

7 The volume of a cube is 588 cm³. Use the method of question **6** to calculate the length of one edge, correct to 2 decimal places.

What's significant?

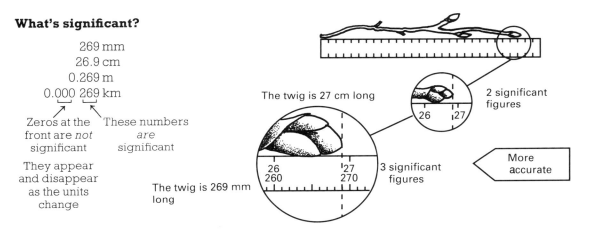

269 mm
26.9 cm
0.269 m
0.000 269 km

Zeros at the front are *not* significant

These numbers *are* significant

They appear and disappear as the units change

The twig is 269 mm long

The twig is 27 cm long

2 significant figures

3 significant figures

More accurate

EXERCISE 4F

---

1 How many significant figures are in each measurement?
  a 37 000 litres   **b** 205 mg   **c** 77.8 kg   **d** 0.009 m
  e 0.707 seconds   **f** 0.000 02 m³   **g** 300.003 g

2 Round these figures to the given number of significant figures.
  a 79 490 (3)   **b** 0.002 088 (1)   **c** 0.999 (2)
  d 5.0099 (4)   **e** 28.0655 (4)

3 A pile of 11 identical books stands 58 cm high.
  a Calculate the thickness of one book.
  b To how many significant figures should you give your answer?

4 Suppose your local Sports Hall is carefully measured to be 58.7 m by 23.6 m.
  a Calculate the area of the floor.
  b The hall is a cuboid in shape and is 6.3 m high. Calculate its volume.

5 A rectangle measures 4.26 m by 0.730 m.
  a Write down the lower and upper limits of these measurements.
  b Calculate the lower and upper limits of its area.

6 In a science experiment the value of $\dfrac{PV}{T}$ for a gas is calculated:

P is its pressure, V its volume and T its temperature in degrees Kelvin (K).
These measurements are taken: $P = 1016\,\text{g/cm}^2$, $V = 348\,\text{cm}^3$ and $T = 212°\text{K}$.

a To how many significant figures should the value of $\dfrac{PV}{T}$ be calculated?

b Calculate the value of $\dfrac{PV}{T}$.

EXERCISE 5F

---

1 Terry has done the following calculations, but they are all wrong. Can you spot his mistakes?

    a $3 \times 5^2 = 225$ **b** $6 + 3 + 1^2 = 100$

    c $8 \times (5 + 3) = 43$ **d** $10 - 1^2 = 81$

    e $(7 + 3) \times (8 - 5) = 75$ **f** $12 + 4 \times 2^3 = 8000$

2 Write down the correct answers in question **1**.

3 Calculate the following, without using a calculator.

    a 2×4^2 **b** $10 + 2^3$ **c** $(4 + 5)^2$ **d** $(16 \div 8)^4$

    e $(40 \div 20) \div 2$ **f** $40 \div (20 \div 2)$ **g** $(6 + 1)^2 - (7 - 1)^2$ **h** $10^3 + 5^3$

    i $6 \times (5 + 1^2)$ **j** $6 \times (5 + 1)^2$ **k** $((4 + 8) \div 6) \div 2$ **l** $((6 - 4) + 5) \times 8$

4 When 2 is input, this function machine calculates $(2 + 3) \times 2 = 10$.

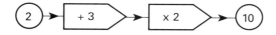

Write out the calculations for these machines:

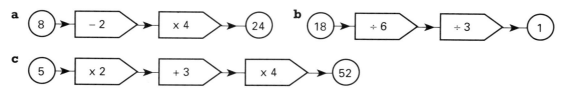

5 Show how you use: (i) brackets   (ii) calculator memory   (iii) another way; to calculate:

    a $\dfrac{48\,000}{757 - 397}$ **b** $\dfrac{64\,000}{357 + 456 + 787}$ **c** $\dfrac{85\,914}{(67 + 19) \times 27}$ **d** $\dfrac{3000}{4.5^2 + 6.5^2}$

EXERCISE 6F

Try all of these without a calculator!

1 a $8+9+7$ **b** $13+11+9$ **c** $7+15-13$ **d** $23-15+11$ **e** $36-17-8$

2 a $6\times5\times4$ **b** $7\times5\times4$ **c** $8\times4\times3$ **d** $6\times6\times6$ **e** $6\times5\times4\times3\times2$

3 a $78+65$ **b** $84+57$ **c** $172+95$ **d** $92-27$ **e** $152-78$

4 a 8×20 **b** 9×70 **c** 6×300 **d** 40×80 **e** 700×700

5 a $80\div40$ **b** $600\div30$ **c** $8000\div400$ **d** $1000\div50$ **e** $60\,000\div30$

6 a $492+68$ **b** $798+216$ **c** $78+92+64$ **d** $612-498$ **e** $704-88$

7 a $5\times17\times4$ **b** $6\times22\times5$ **c** $25\times37\times4$ **d** $40\times38\times5$ **e** $15\times26\times4$

8 a $8\times7+2\times7$ **b** $9\times6-2\times6$ **c** $39\times5+11\times5$ **d** $27\times16-7\times16$

9 a 872×3 **b** 36×42 **c** 43×87 **d** 635×39 **e** 748×689

10 a $408\div12$ **b** $864\div16$ **c** $1184\div37$ **d** $1632\div24$ **e** $1786\div47$

2 ALL ABOUT ANGLES

EXERCISE 1F

1 The Leaning Tower of Pisa slopes at an angle of 85° to the ground. How many degrees is it from the vertical?

2 What angle must the lever be turned through to be:
a vertical   **b** horizontal?

3 The pendulum swings through 90°. Calculate y when it is:
a half of x **b** double x **c** three times x **d** four times x
e one and a half times x.

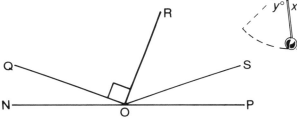

4 $\angle NOQ = \angle POS$
$\angle ROS = 2 \times \angle POS$
Calculate the size of $\angle NOQ$.

5 Find two pairs of complementary angles in the diagram on the right.
Explain your answers.

6 What is the complement of:
a 15°   **b** $y°$ **c** $2a°$ **d** $(45-y)°$
e $(80-x)°$?

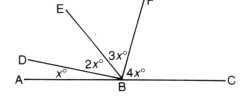

7 a What is the angle between the hands of a clock at five minutes past twelve?
b How many minutes must pass before the hands of the clock are at right angles? (Give your answer to the nearest half minute.)

EXERCISE 2F

1 What angles can the lever be turned through to be:
a horizontal   **b** vertical?

2 Carefully measure these angles to find which pairs are supplementary:

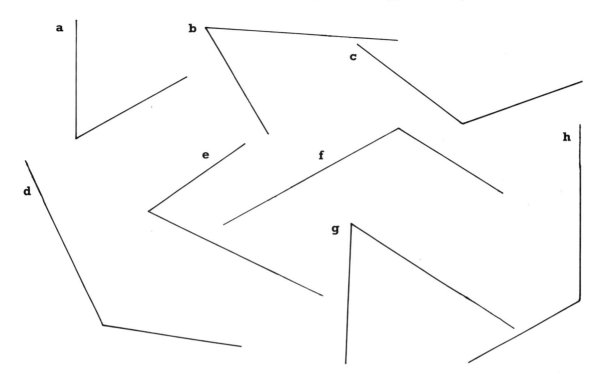

3 AC and DG are straight lines.
  a Name the supplement of:
    (i) $\angle$ ABE   (ii) $\angle$ DBE   (iii) $\angle$ FBG
  b Name two angles which are the
    supplement of:
    (i) $\angle$ ABD   (ii) $\angle$ CBG
  c Calculate the size of $\angle$ ABG.

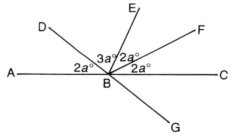

4 a A car is travelling at a steady 30 km/h. It
    accelerates to 120 km/h. Through what
    angle does the needle turn?
  b Repeat **a** for the car accelerating from
    these speeds to 120 km/h:
    (i) 20 km/h   (ii) 50 km/h   (iii) 80 km/h
    (iv) 110 km/h.

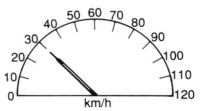

5 What is the supplement of:
  a 80°   **b** $x°$ **c** $2x°$ **d** $(90-2y)°$ **e** $(100+a)°$?

6 The minute and hour hands of a clock form a straight angle at 6 o'clock. When do the
hands next form a straight angle? (Give your answer to the nearest half minute.)

EXERCISE 3F

1 Two rods cross as shown.

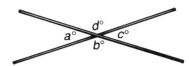

    a Write down as many equations as you can connecting a, b, c
       and d (e.g. $a+b = 180$).
    b Angle $a°$ is decreased by 30°. What effect does this have on the other three angles?
    c Angle $c°$ is doubled. What effect does this have on the other angles?

2 GH, KL and IJ are diameters of the circle.
   Calculate the value of x.

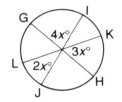

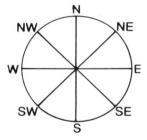

3 How many pairs of vertically opposite angles can you find?
Name them.

4 a How many pairs of vertically opposite angles are there of:
      (i) 45° (ii) 90° (iii) 135°?
    b Repeat **a** for a 16-point compass.

EXERCISE 4F

1 Copy the diagram, and fill in the sizes of as many angles as you
can using *only* the fact that corresponding angles are equal.

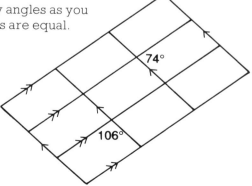

2

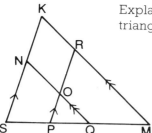

Explain why each angle of triangle NSQ is equal to an angle of triangle PRM.

3 A corner is cut off this rectangular metal plate.
Copy the diagram.
By drawing a suitable line parallel to AX, calculate the size of ∠ABC.

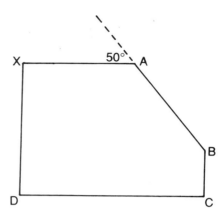

4

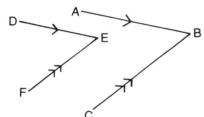

Show that ∠ABC = ∠DEF.
No tracing paper, protractor or scissors allowed.

5 A snooker ball rebounds from the cushion at the same angle at which it strikes it.
Calculate a, b, . . .

a
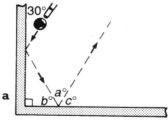

b
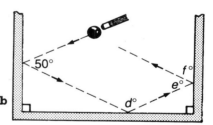

EXERCISE 5F

---

1 Find the sizes of:
   a ∠KON   **b** ∠OKN   **c** ∠KNO.

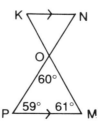

2

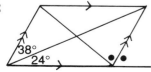

The sign '●' denotes equal angles.
Copy the diagram and fill in the sizes of as many angles as you can.

3 Calculate the sizes of all the angles in the diagram.

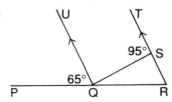

4  Calculate the sizes of the unmarked angles.

5 a Sketch the diagram.
   b How many triangles are there?
   c Mark in the angles of all the triangles in terms of a, b and c.
   d What do you notice about the sum of the angles of each triangle?

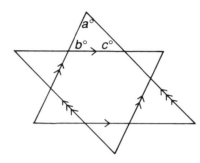

6 Copy the diagram and calculate x and y.
You will need to draw another parallel line to help you.

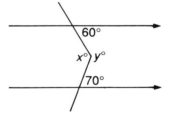

7 A telegraph pole stands vertically at the roadside. The road slopes at 8° to the horizontal. Calculate the acute angle between the pole and the road.

8 Calculate a, b, c, d and e, and f, g, h, j and k

a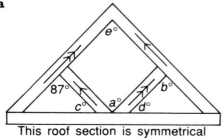
This roof section is symmetrical

b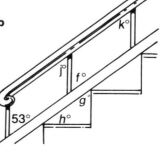

EXERCISE 6F

1 Write down the numbers for as many *pairs* of complementary, supplementary, vertically opposite, corresponding and alternate angles as you can find in the diagrams.

a

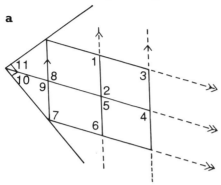

b

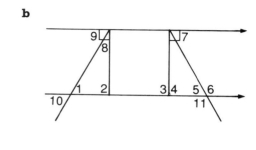

2 **a** Copy the regular hexagon.
  b Using only vertically opposite, corresponding and alternate angles, mark in as many angles of $a°$ and $b°$ as you can.

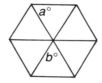

3 Calculate a, b, c, d, e, f and g, h, i, j
  a

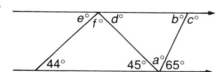

  b

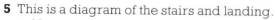

4

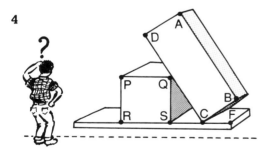

This piece of modern sculpture, 'The Cube and Cuboid,' is assembled on site in the gallery. The sculptor has given instructions that $\angle BCF$ should be 38°.
  a Name pairs of angles which are:
     (i) supplementary   (ii) complementary.
  b Calculate the sizes of:
     (i) $\angle BCR$ (ii) $\angle QCR$ (iii) $\angle DQP$

5 This is a diagram of the stairs and landing.
  a Name three sets of acute alternate angles.
  b Name a pair of obtuse alternate angles.
  c $\angle HIF = 55°$. Copy the diagram and fill in the sizes of as many angles as you can.

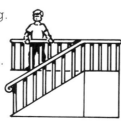

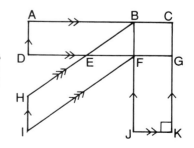

3 LETTERS AND NUMBERS

EXERCISE 1F

1 Write in a shorter form:
   a $y+y$ **b** $y \times y$ **c** $m+m+m$ **d** $m \times m \times m$ **e** $4a+a$
   f $4a \times a$ **g** $3b+2b$ **h** $3b \times 2b$ **i** $6c-5c$ **j** $3d-d$
   k $3 \times n-5$ **l** $2 \times k \times 5$ **m** $t \times 6 \times t$ **n** $2a \times 3a \times 4a$ **o** $5 \times c \times 3 \times d$

2 Write out in full:
   a 6^3 **b** 10^4 **c** y^5 **d** $3s^2$ **e** $5n^3$ **f** $2a^2b^2$

3 Combine the terms on these cards firstly by adding them and
secondly by multiplying them *in pairs*. Write down your answers
methodically, for example:
$b+2b = \ldots, b \times 2b = \ldots$

4 Write down the numbers and letters that should go in the empty circles. All the diagrams
deal with addition.

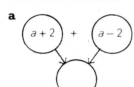 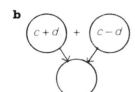 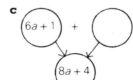 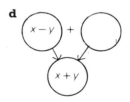

5 Write down the numbers and letters that should go in the empty circles. All the diagrams
deal with multiplication.

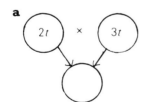 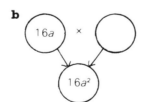 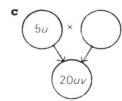 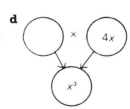

6 When the spinners have stopped, the lowest terms are multiplied
together.
   a List all possible products.
   b Which products are you:
     (i) most likely to have   (ii) least likely to have?

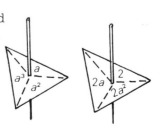

Investigation

1 Investigate values of t that make: **a** $t^2 = 2t$ **b** t^2 greater than $2t$ **c** t^2 less than $2t$

2 Investigate values of x that make: **a** $x^2 = 2^x$ **b** x^2 greater than 2^x **c** x^2 less than 2^x.

EXERCISE 2F

1 | $x = 2$ and $y = 7$ | Find the value of:

a $x+y$ **b** $y-x$ **c** $2(x+y)$ **d** $3(y-x)$
e $x(x+2)$ **f** $y(y-x)$ **g** $3(x+7)$ **h** $x(y-2)$
i $(y+2)(y-2)$ **j** $(x+1)(y-1)$ **k** $x(x+3)+4$ **l** $y(y-3)+x$
m $y(x+1)$ **n** $(x+y)(y-x)$ **o** $(2x+y)(x+3)$ **p** $(5x+y)(5x-y)$

2 $a = 2$ and $b = 4$. Find the value of:
a b^2+1 **b** b^2-3 **c** a^2+2 **d** $(3a)^2$
e $2a^2$ **f** $3a^2+1$ **g** $(2a)^2-1$ **h** $10-a^2$
i $18-3a^2$ **j** $(a+1)^2$ **k** $(b-2)^2$ **l** $(a+b)^2$
m $(b-a)^2$ **n** $2(a+2)^2$ **o** $3(b-2)^2$ **p** $(8-b)^2$
q $3(7-a)^2$ **r** $2(a^2+1)$ **s** $5(b^2-5)$ **t** $a^2(a+1)$
u $b^2(b-1)$ **v** $2(a+1)(b-1)$ **w** $2(b+1)^2(a+1)$ **x** $(a^2+1)^2$

3 $p = 1$, $q = 2$ and $r = 3$. Find the value of:
a q^2+2q **b** r^2+2r+1 **c** $(r+1)^2$
d $q(q+2)$ **e** $(2p+1)(p+1)$ **f** $(p+q)^2+q^2$
g $2p^2+3p+1$ **h** $p^2+2pq+2q^2$ **i** $pq(p+q)$
j $(2p+q)^2$ **k** p^2q+pq^2 **l** $4p^2+4pq+q^2$

Challenge

By testing other values of p, q and r, pair the expressions in question **3** in possible equal expressions.

4 $x = 2$, $y = 3$ and $z = 6$. Calculate:

a $\frac{1}{3}(x+4)$ **b** $\frac{1}{3}(y+z)$ **c** $\dfrac{z-x}{2}$ **d** $\dfrac{2y+3x}{z}$

e $\dfrac{y^2+z^2}{x+y}$ **f** $\dfrac{2z^2+3y}{z+y}$ **g** $\dfrac{2(z-y)^2}{y^2}$ **h** $\dfrac{(2y)^2}{2y^2}$

EXERCISE 3F

1 Write down an expression for the distance between villages:
     a A and C   **b** B and D   **c** A and D

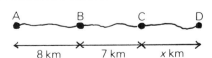

2 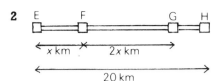 Write down an expression for the distance between towns:
a E and G   **b** G and H   **c** F and H

3 Write down an expression for the distance between stations:
a I and K   **b** K and L   **c** J and L
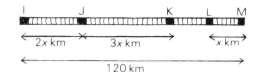

4 Find expressions for the lengths (in centimetres) of the unmarked straws.

a 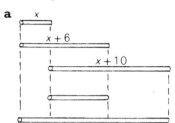   **b** 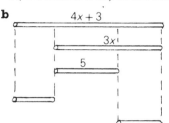   **c**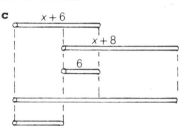

5 Jessie swims each of four lengths of the pool in t seconds. She fails to beat the school record by 1 second. Find a formula for the school record time, T seconds.

6 Five pieces of wire, each $3d$ cm long, are cut from a wire which is 2 m long. Find a formula for the length of wire L cm, that is left.

7 Make a formula for the perimeter P of each pane of glass and for the whole window frame. Lengths are in centimetres.

a

(figure: rectangle $6a$ wide, $3a$ high, with $3a$ and a marked)

b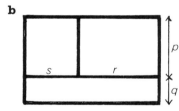

c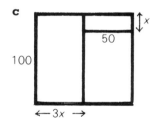

8 A rectangular conservatory floor is covered with square tiles of side s cm. There are 25 rows of tiles, each containing 10 tiles. Find a formula for the perimeter P of the floor.

9 Make a formula for the perimeter of each rectangular part of the garden. Measurements are in metres.

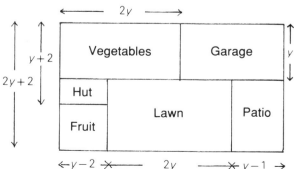

10 Make a formula for the area (A) of each shape. The lengths are in centimetres.

a
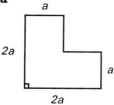

b
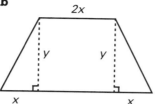

c
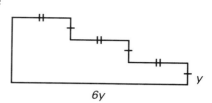

11 A cube is x cm long. Find formulae for:
 a the total length of its edges   **b** its surface area   **c** its volume.

12 a Find a formula for the volume of this oil tank. Lengths are in metres.
 b What is the depth of oil when the tank is half full?

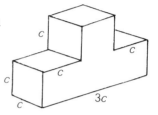

EXERCISE 4F

Calculate the total length of logs in each pile (in metres), before and after cutting. Then equate the two expressions.

Example

6 logs cut

(i)   Before cutting, $6(x+2)$

(ii)   After cutting, $6x+12$

$$6(x+2)=6x+12$$

1

2

3

4

5
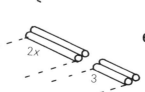

6
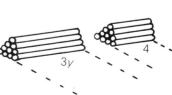

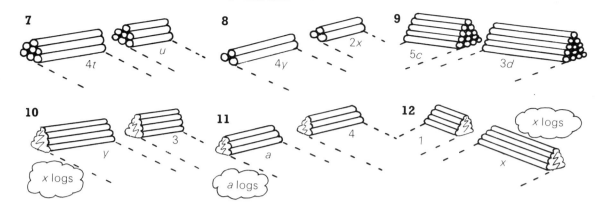

EXERCISE 5F

1 Remove the brackets and simplify where possible:

  a $4 + x(1 - x)$
  b $m(m - n) + m(m + n)$

  c $3(x + 4) + 2(x - 1)$
  d $y(y^2 + 3)$
  e $a(a^2 - 5)$

  f $b(2b^2 + b)$
  g $c(5 - c^2)$
  h $x(x^2 + 2) + x(x^2 - 2)$

  i $a(b - 3) + b(a + 3)$
  j $5(x - y) + x(2 + y)$
  k $y^2(y - 1) + y(y^2 + 1)$

2 Ian was asked to remove brackets from $(x + 2)(x + 3)$.

He reasoned: $(x + 2)(x + 3) = x(x + 3) + 2(x + 3)$
$$= x^2 + 3x + 2x + 6$$
$$= x^2 + 5x + 6$$

He checked, choosing (at random) $x = 5$:

$$(x + 2)(x + 3) = (5 + 2)(5 + 3) = 7 \times 8 = 56$$

$$x^2 + 5x + 6 = 5^2 + 5 \times 5 + 6 = 25 + 25 + 6 = 56 \ldots \text{ The answers agreed!}$$

Use his method to remove brackets from these expressions (check your answer, choosing a value for x):

  a $(x + 1)(x + 2)$
  b $(x + 5)(x + 2)$
  c $(y + 2)(y + 2)$

  d $(2x + 1)(3x + 3)$
  e $(x + y)(x + y)$
  f $(3x + 4)(5x + 1)$

3 Try to extend the method in question **2** to remove brackets from:

  a $(x + 1)(x + y + 1)$
  b $(x + 1)(x^2 + x + 1)$

Investigation   Remove brackets:

$$(x + 1) = \ldots \ldots \ldots \ldots \ldots x + 1$$
$$(x + 1)(x + 1) = \ldots \ldots \ldots \ldots$$
$$(x + 1)(x + 1)(x + 1) = \ldots \ldots \ldots$$
$$(x + 1)(x + 1)(x + 1)(x + 1) = \ldots \ldots$$
$$(x + 1)(x + 1)(x + 1)(x + 1)(x + 1) = \ldots$$

Describe any patterns that you see in your answers.
Try to find out about Pascal's Triangle. What has it to do with your answers?

4 MAKING SENSE OF STATISTICS 1

EXERCISE 1F

1 The graph shows Maxie Rae's speed during the first lap of a Grand Prix race.
   a What is her maximum speed? For how long does she maintain this speed?
   b How many tight bends are there on the circuit? Explain your answer.
   c Maxie uses top gear at speeds over 160 km/h. How long is she in top gear during the lap?

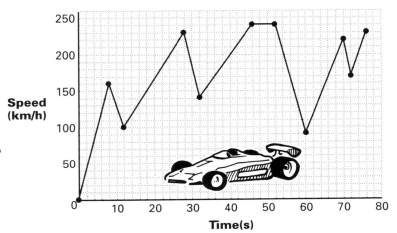

2 The graph shows the number of births and deaths in Newtown each year from 1980–1989.

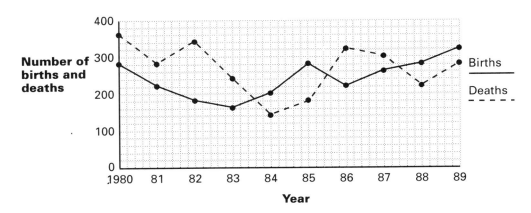

   a In which years did the population increase?
   b In which year was there the greatest increase? What was this increase?
   c How did the population of Newtown in 1989 compare with the population in 1980?

3 The graph shows the monthly sales of milk in the supermarket.

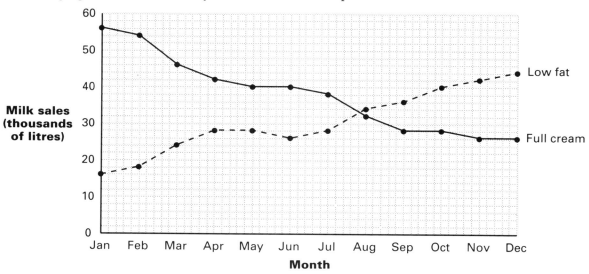

a What were the total sales of milk in March?
b Calculate the total sales of full cream milk for the year.
c What fraction of the month's sales was low fat in: (i) January   (ii) December?
d Write a sentence or two about the two line graphs, explaining any reason for the way
they look.

EXERCISE 2F

1 What is wrong with these graphs?

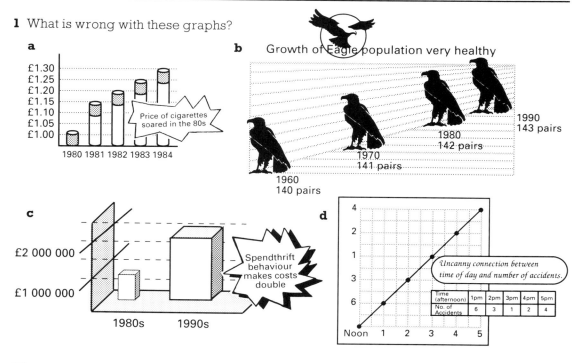

2 Draw this graph on squared paper, and comment on the rate of growth of the profit.

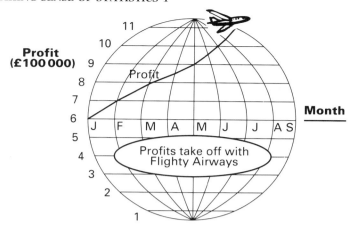

EXERCISE 3F

1 A hotel chain has branches in three villages on a holiday island. Over the four summer months each hotel keeps a record of bookings.

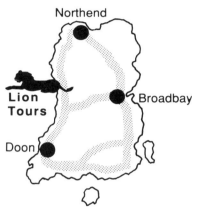

Northend				Lion Tours
Week	Jun	Jul	Aug	Sep
1	15	14	17	16
2	14	15	18	21
3	12	13	17	23
4	21	23	12	15

Broadbay				Lion Tours
Week	Jun	Jul	Aug	Sep
1	17	15	12	17
2	20	12	15	20
3	18	15	13	20
4	15	18	17	17

Doon				Lion Tours
Week	Jun	Jul	Aug	Sep
1	19	14	15	17
2	11	16	12	18
3	13	14	13	16
4	11	20	10	14

Which hotel had the best mean booking:
a over the four months
b during the height of the season (July and August)?

2

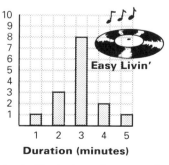

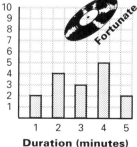

The graphs indicate how long tracks are, to the nearest minute, on two CDs. For example, on the *Easy Livin'* CD there is one track of one minute, three tracks of two minutes, etc.
a What is the mean duration of a track on the *Easy Livin'* CD?
b Compare this CD with the *Fortunate* CD with respect to track length.

3

Sing a song of sixpence,
A pocket full of rye;
Four and twenty blackbirds,
Baked in a pie.

When the pie was opened,
The birds began to sing;
Was not that a dainty dish,
To set before the king?

I had a duck-billed platypus when I was
up at Trinity
With whom I soon discovered a
remarkable affinity.
He used to live in lodgings with myself
and Arthur Purvis,
And we all went up together for the
Diplomatic service.
I had a certain confidence, I own, in his
ability;
He mastered all the subjects with
remarkable facility;
And Purvis, though more dubious,
agreed that he was clever,
But no one else imagined he had any
chance whatever.

These are the first **eight** lines of two poems. For each, find:
a the mean number of words per line
b the mean number of letters per word.
Why would you say that the second poem is probably not meant for the same readers as the first?

Extract from 'I had a duck-billed platypus' by Patrick Barrington, reproduced from *Punch*, 23 August 1933.

EXERCISE 4F

1 The diagram gives an indication of the weights, to the nearest 5 kg, of all the pupils in Sandra's class.
   a Which is the modal weight?
   b By writing the list of weights out like 55, 55, 60, 60, 60, 60, 60, 65, . . . , calculate:
      (i) the median weight
      (ii) the mean weight
      (iii) the range of weights.

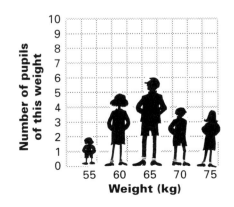

2 When they ended their holidays in a holiday camp, people were asked which day of the week had been their favourite with regard to camp entertainment.
The charts show the results for the first and last weeks of July.

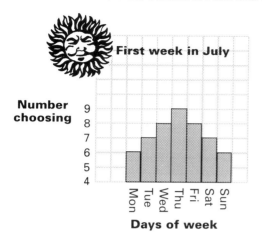 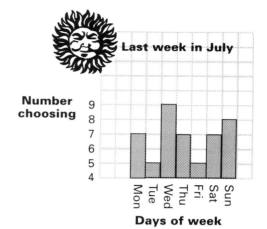

a For each week identify the modal day.
b (i) What was the mean number of votes for a Monday?
    (ii) Work out the mean number of votes for each day of the week.
c (i) What was the lowest number of votes cast for a day?
    (ii) What was the range of votes cast per day?

3 Five coins were thrown in the air. When they landed the number of heads visible was counted.
The chart indicates the results of 32 such experiments.

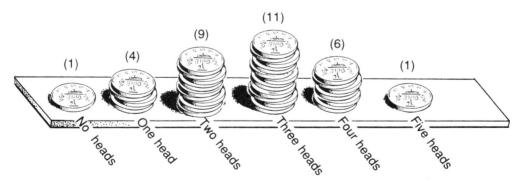

a What was the modal number of heads to show?
b Calculate the mean number of heads in the above experiments.
c Take five coins and perform the experiment.
Try the experiment with 1, 2, 3, 4, and 6 coins.
Look at this triangle of numbers.
Does it bear any relation to your results?

```
            1    1
          1    2    1
        1    3    3    1
      1    4    6    4    1
    1    5   10   10    5    1
  1    6   15   20   15    6    1
```

5 FRACTIONS, DECIMALS AND PERCENTAGES

EXERCISE 1F

1 Arrange these numbers in order, smallest first:
0.025, two hundredths, 0.019, twenty two thousandths.

2 Multiply each number by (i) 100 and (ii) by 10 000:
   a 0.007   **b** 0.25   **c** 0.000 26

3 Divide each number (i) by 100 and (ii) by 10 000:
   a 40   **b** 3700   **c** 65 200

4 A pile of paper is 7.8 cm high. Each sheet is 0.01 cm thick.
   a How many sheets of paper are in the pile?
   b What would be the height of a pile of 500 sheets?

5 Best Brew tea bags are sold in two sizes of pack, 580 g for £3.45 and 360 g for £2.35. Which is the better buy?

6 Calculate the charges on this gas bill, to the nearest penny.

Kilowatts used	Pence per kilowatt	Charge
1523	1.507	a
Standing charge period	Pence per day	
82 days	10.3p	b
	Total	c

7 Find the entries in the blanks on this gas bill. Give your answer to the nearest whole number.

Kilowatts used	Pence per unit	Charge
c	1.507	b
Standing charge period	Pence per day	
a days	10.3p	£8.96
	Total	£35.74

EXERCISE 2F

1 What do you call:
  a $\frac{1}{7}$ of a week   **b** $\frac{1}{100}$ of a metre   **c** $\frac{1}{1000}$ of a kilogram   **d** $\frac{1}{3600}$ of an hour?

2 Simplify these fractions: **a** $\frac{10}{12}$ **b** $\frac{18}{24}$ **c** $\frac{6}{18}$ **d** $\frac{12}{50}$ **e** $\frac{40}{48}$ **f** $\frac{28}{42}$

3 Calculate: **a** $\frac{7}{10}$ of £3   **b** $\frac{2}{5}$ of £3   **c** $\frac{5}{8}$ of £32   **d** $\frac{5}{12}$ of £72

4 What fraction of a circle, in simplest form, is each of these parts?

a   90°   **b**   110°   **c** 75° **d** 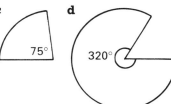 320°   **e**   150°

5 Calculate:
  a 10% of £2.50   **b** 15% of £80   **c** 8% of £300   **d** 40% of £6.40

6 At a rugby ground which has a capacity of 2400, there are seats for 840 people. When the ground is full, calculate the percentage of people who are: **a** sitting   **b** standing.

7 Which is greater and by how much?   **a** 18% of £250 or $\frac{3}{20}$ of £280   **b** $12\frac{1}{2}$% of £6.80 or $\frac{11}{12}$ of 96p

EXERCISE 3F

1 A fruiterer bought 500 apples for £55 and wanted to sell them at 70p for five.
  a What could be expected: (i) as the total profit   (ii) as the profit per apple?
  b But 7% of the stock was damaged and could not be sold.
    (i) What was the total profit on the deal now?
    (ii) If an allowance for the damage had been made how might the stock have been
        priced so as to maintain the original total expected profit?

2 Des sells discontinued lines of old records at the market:
  'Recent Hits'—2 for £3;   'Golden Oldies'—3 for £2.
  He buys 300 of each kind at £45 per 100.
  a What profit should he make on all of the: (i) Recent Hits   (ii) Golden Oldies?
  b What is the total profit?
    The records arrive all mixed up so he decides to sell them as:
    'Disco Selection'—5 for £5.
    'Same profit' Des thinks.
  c Calculate his profit now. Investigate why this is not the same as previously (in part **b**).

3 A car sales agent starts a 'Dutch auction' on a car.

   a Calculate the price of the car on Tuesday, Wednesday, Thursday and Friday.

   b The garage is open 7 days a week. On which day will the car be offered at less than half of Monday's price? What is this price?

4 Study this calculation of bank interest. Notice that the interest is calculated each year on complete £s (pounds sterling).

```
AMOUNT IN BANK AT START          =  £ 127.30
8% INTEREST :  0.08 × 127        =     10.16
AMOUNT IN BANK AT END OF YEAR 1  =    137.46
8% INTEREST : 0.08 × 137         =     10.96
AMOUNT IN BANK AT END OF YEAR 2  =    148.42
               TOTAL INTEREST    =  £  21.12
```

Calculate the interest on:
   a £273 at 12% per annum over 3 years
   b £500 at 7% per annum over 4 years.

5 Mr Boyd marks Janey's exam paper and awards the mark, 66%.
However when he checks his marking he finds he missed a question and the actual mark is 69%. Calculate the percentage error, correct to 1 decimal place.

6 Shelly orders a square mirror of side 30 cm. The actual mirror she receives is 10% too long in one direction and 10% too short in the other.
   a Is the area of the mirror larger or smaller than the one she ordered?
   b What is the percentage error compared to the one she ordered?

EXERCISE 4F

1 Change the following (i) to fractions in their simplest form, and (ii) to decimal fractions:
   a 32%   **b** 14%   **c** 65%   **d** 8%   **e** 12.5%   **f** 2%

2 Arrange in order, smallest first: 36%, $\frac{19}{50}$, 0.35, $\frac{74}{200}$

3 Which is greater?
   a 72% of £36, or 36% of £72   **b** $\frac{5}{8}$ of 35 cm, or 15 cm ÷ 0.64

4 Change the following   (i) to decimal fractions, correct to 3 decimal places, then (ii) to percentages, correct to 1 decimal place, where necessary:
a $\frac{5}{6}$ **b** $\frac{5}{8}$ **c** $\frac{3}{7}$ **d** $\frac{7}{10}$ **e** $\frac{1}{25}$ **f** $\frac{3}{40}$

5 These four jigsaw pieces can fit together. They are all equal—the same number expressed as a percentage, as a decimal, as a fraction of 100 and as a fraction in its simplest form. Copy the jigsaws below and complete them in the same way.

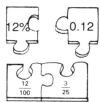

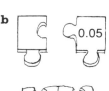 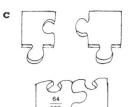 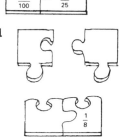

6 Change these numbers   (i) to percentages, and   (ii) to fractions, in their simplest form:
a 0.6   **b** 0.19   **c** 0.885   **d** 0.08   **e** 0.72   **f** 0.003

7 Find the fractions which are equal to;
a 0.222 . . .   **b** 0.333 . . .   **c** 0.0909 . . .   **d** 0.1333 . . .

EXERCISE 5F

1 Forty people were asked to name World Cup Football Teams they liked (apart from their own). Copy and complete the pie chart showing percentages and angles. Use a protractor to draw the 'slices'.

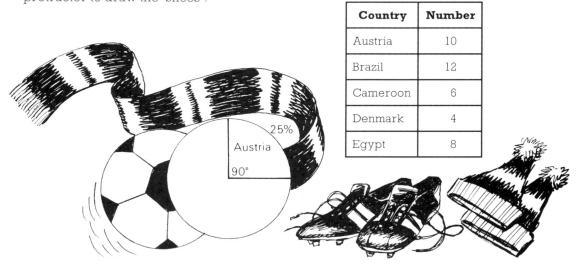

Country	Number
Austria	10
Brazil	12
Cameroon	6
Denmark	4
Egypt	8

2 It is estimated that six gases contribute to the 'greenhouse' effect on the earth's atmosphere in the following percentages. Illustrate the given information in a pie chart.

Carbon dioxide	Methane	CFCs	Ozone	Nitrous oxide
50%	18%	14%	12%	6%

3 Deirdre's temperature rose from 36.8°C to 37.2°C.
Calculate the percentage increase, correct to 1 decimal place.

4 Jamil grows tomato seeds in two types of soil, A and B.
In type A, $\frac{7}{8}$ of the seeds germinate and in type B $\frac{5}{6}$ of the seeds are successful.
a Calculate the success rate of each type as a percentage, correct to 1 decimal place.
b Which type is more successful and what is the percentage difference?

5 In 1980 the costs involved in building a house were:
salaries and wages £45 000, materials £30 000, other £15 000.
By 1990, the costs had increased by 120%, 90% and 85% respectively.
Calculate: **a** the cost of the house in: (i) 1980   (ii) 1990
　　　　　　 b the percentage increase in the cost between 1980 and 1990, to the nearest 1%.

6 A bike from the Cykal Company loses 20% of its current value every year. In 1990 it cost £200 new. Calculate its value in:
a 1991　　**b** 1992 (it loses 20% of its 1991 value)　　**c** 1993

7 Superstrain Filter clears 75% of the impurities in water. Water is safe for car radiators if it contains less than 1% of impurities. How many times must water be filtered to make it safe if it starts off with 64 g of impurities in 100 g of water?

8 The table shows the salt content in various sources of water.
15‰ means 15 per thousand $= \frac{15}{1000} = \frac{1.5}{100} = 1.5\%$
a Write each salinity as a fraction and as a percentage.
b Find the salinity of a pail of water which is a mixture of equal amounts of the four sources.

Water	Salinity
Sea	35‰
River	0.16‰
Dead Sea	192‰
Salt Lake	203‰

6 DISTANCES AND DIRECTIONS

EXERCISE 1F

1 The helicopter is 120 m above the water. It sights the tug at an angle of depression of 38°. Make a scale drawing, and find the direct distance of a line from the helicopter to the tug.

2

The angle of depression of the bottom of the hill (F) from the top (T) is 62°. The angle of depression of the buoy (B) from the top of the hill is 35°.
The buoy is 60 metres from the foot of the hill. Use a scale drawing to find the height of the hill.

3 A hot air balloon is 500 m above the buoy at an angle of elevation of 40° from the motor boat. From the balloon a lighthouse has an angle of depression of 50°. If the boat, buoy and lighthouse are in a straight line, in this order, find the length of that line.

4 Three spacecraft are equidistant from each other, 13 000 km apart. They need to meet as quickly as possible. They all have the same maximum speed of 1 km/s. Use a scale drawing to determine the minimum time required for all three spacecraft to come to the same point (to the nearest minute).

EXERCISE 2F

1 Cheryl sets out from the cabin, walking 8 kilometres north-east before changing direction and walking 8 kilometres south-east. She then walks in a south-westerly direction until she is due south of the cabin before returning to it. Make a scale drawing of her route and find how far she walked altogether.

2 **a** The route for a marathon walk is:
START → 5 km SW → 5 km W → 5 km NW → 5 km N → 5 km NE → 5 km E → 5 km SE → 5 km S, FINISH
The 'junior' marathon route starts from the same point, then:
2.5 km SW → 2.5 km W → 2.5 km NW → 2.5 km N → 2.5km NE → 2.5 km E → 2.5 km SE → 2.5 km S, FINISH
Make a scale drawing of the two routes on the same diagram.
   b What shape is each route?

3 On a 16-point compass, what angle is between:
   a NNE and E   **b** WSW and SSW   **c** NNW and ESE   **d** WSW and ESE?

EXERCISE 3F

1 The diagram shows the position of craters around the landing site of Apollo 12 on the moon's surface. Use tracing paper, ruler and protractor to measure the bearings of the craters from the Apollo landing site. All angles should be measured clockwise from the direction shown by the arrow.

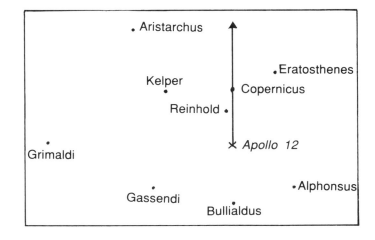

2 a Write down the bearing of B from A in each of these:

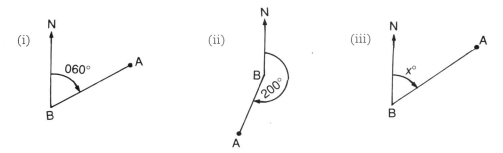

b What is the bearing in (iii) if $x°$ lies between 090° and 180°, or between 180° and 360°?

3 The point B is equidistant from points A and C.
   a The bearing of B from A is 050°.
   The bearing of C from B is 120°.
   What is the bearing of C from A?
   b The bearing of B from A is 080°.
   The bearing of C from B is 040°.
   What is the bearing of C from A?
   c Investigate the bearing of C from A when the bearing of B from A is $x°$ and the bearing of C from B is $y°$.

EXERCISE 4F

1 Port B is 15 km due east of port A. A yacht leaves A on a bearing of 048° and sails for 6 km. Changing course it goes a further 8 km on a bearing of 149° and anchors. A second yacht leaves B on a bearing of 308° and sails for 4 km.
Use a scale drawing to give the second yacht a bearing and distance to meet the first yacht at its anchorage.

2 A ship sailing on a course of 050° sees a lighthouse on a bearing of 040°. Three kilometres further on the bearing of the lighthouse is 023°.
   a Make a scale drawing.
   b How much further must the ship travel to reach the point of closest approach?
   c How close does it get?

3 *The dance of the bee.*

A bee returns to the hive after discovering a new site of flowers. It does a 'dance' on the honeycomb. Part of the dance is a waggle-run.

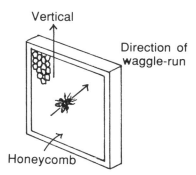

The other bees learn the direction of the waggle-run, which can be described by the bearing from the vertical.

Once outside the hive the bees use this bearing to find the direction of the new flowers. But they now take the bearing to be the bearing of the flowers from the direction of the sun.

From the speed of the waggle-run the bees can tell the distance of the new flowers from the hive.

The graph shows the relationship.

a Measure the bearing of the waggle-run at the beginning of the question. Six runs are made in a minute. Use the graph to find the distance to the flowers and use the diagram on the page opposite to check that the dance leads to Knotweed flowers.

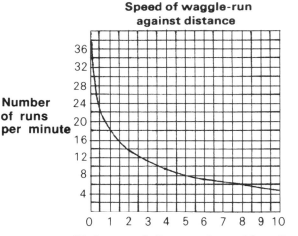

Speed of waggle-run against distance

Number of runs per minute

Distance of flowers from hive (km)

b To which flowers do these runs lead?

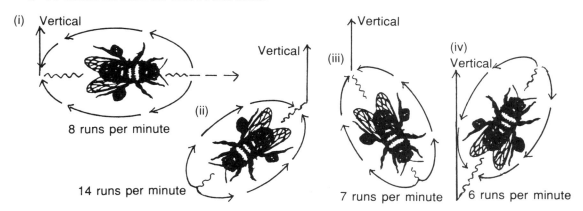

(i) Vertical

8 runs per minute

(ii) 14 runs per minute

(iii) Vertical
7 runs per minute

(iv) Vertical
6 runs per minute

Position of various flowers around the hive

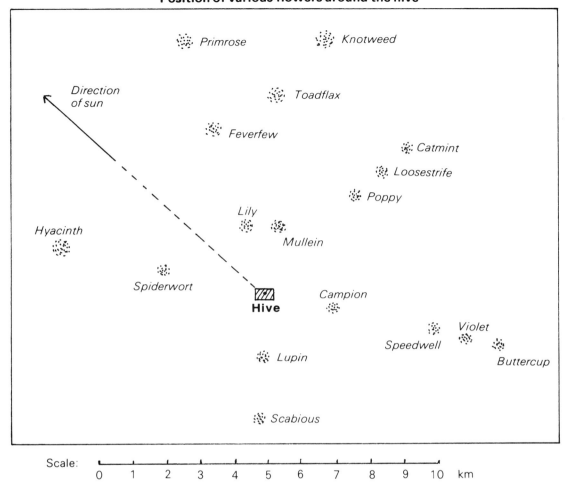

Scale:

0   1   2   3   4   5   6   7   8   9   10   km

c Choose some other flower beds and draw diagrams of the run that would tell the other bees where the flowers are. Remember to describe the speed of the run. Ask a friend to find the flowers from your data.

7 POSITIVE AND NEGATIVE NUMBERS

EXERCISE 1F

1 Geophysical data such as the heights of hills, mountains and clouds are measured from sea-level. Features below sea-level are often given 'negative heights'.

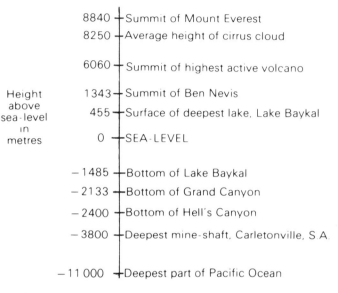

Height above sea-level in metres

8840	Summit of Mount Everest
8250	Average height of cirrus cloud
6060	Summit of highest active volcano
1343	Summit of Ben Nevis
455	Surface of deepest lake, Lake Baykal
0	SEA-LEVEL
−1485	Bottom of Lake Baykal
−2133	Bottom of Grand Canyon
−2400	Bottom of Hell's Canyon
−3800	Deepest mine-shaft, Carletonville, S.A.
−11 000	Deepest part of Pacific Ocean

a How much higher is Mount Everest than Ben Nevis?

b How much deeper is Hell's Canyon than Grand Canyon?

c How much deeper is the Pacific Ocean than the mine-shaft?

d How deep is Lake Baykal?

e What is the difference in distance between the height of Mount Everest and the depth of the Pacific Ocean?

f How much higher above sea-level is the summit of the volcano than the bottom of the mine-shaft is below sea-level?

2 The table shows the average daily maximum temperatures in January in some of the world's hottest and coldest capitals.
London is included for comparison.

a How many degrees warmer is Asunçion than Ulan Batur?

b What is the difference between the temperature in London and in:
  (i) Ascunçion   (ii) Nicosia
  (iii) Moscow   (iv) Ulan Batur?

c Compare the temperatures in Ottawa and Moscow.

d Compare Ulan Batur's July temperature of 21.6°C with its January temperature.

Capital	Country	Temp. (°C)
Asunçion	Paraguay	35
Conakry	Guinea	34.3
San Salvador	El Salvador	32.2
Wellington	New Zealand	20.5
Nicosia	Cyprus	14.9
London	England	6.3
Ottawa	Canada	−6.5
Moscow	CIS	−9.3
Ulan Batur	Mongolia	−18.8

3 Verkhoyansk in the CIS has the Earth's greatest temperature range, from $-48.5°C$ to $18.3°C$. How many degrees is this?

4 The coldest temperature ever recorded on Earth was $-88.3°C$ at Vostok in the Antarctic on August 24, 1960. How many degrees is this below the January temperature in:
   a Ulan Batur   **b** London?

5 a The image of $(3, 1)$ under reflection in the dotted line is $(3, -5)$. Copy the diagram.
  b Plot the points in the table and their images.
  c Copy and complete the table.

Point	Image
$(1, 2)$	
$(-2, 0)$	
$(5, -6)$	
$(-4, -3)$	
$(4, 20)$	
(a, b)	

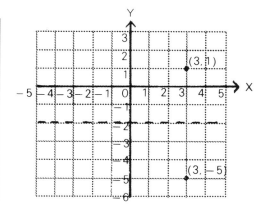

6 a Draw a dotted line through the points $(-8, 8)$, $(0, 0)$ and $(7, -7)$.
  b Plot the points R$(6, -2)$, S$(0, 7)$, T$(-3, 7)$ and U$(-3, 4)$ then join them up in order. What shape is RSTU?
  c Plot the images of R, S, T, U under reflection in the dotted line and join them up in order. Write down the coordinates of the image points. Compare them with the coordinates of R, S, T and U.

EXERCISE 2F

Reminder

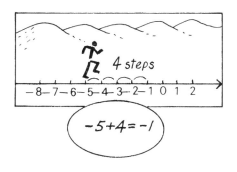

$-5+4 = -1$

1 Calculate:
  a $-2+3$ **b** $-2+1$ **c** $-4+8$
  d $-5+5$ **e** $0+1$ **f** $-6+0$
  g $-9+8$ **h** $-8+9$ **i** $-1+11$
  j $-15+7$ **k** $-24+15$ **l** $-30+21$
  m $-3x+2x$ **n** $-5y+y$ **o** $-2a+4a$
  p $-b+6b$ **q** $-8c+8c$ **r** $-4d+d$

2 Use the 'cover up' method to find the number that x stands for in each equation.
  a $x+3 = 1$ **b** $x+7 = 2$ **c** $-1+x = 0$ **d** $-5+x = -4$
  e $-13+x = 9$ **f** $-8+x = -1$ **g** $x+4 = -3$ **h** $x+1 = -4$
  i $x+6 = -5$ **j** $-11+2x = -1$ **k** $-15+3x = 3$ **l** $-7+2x = -1$

3 Terri's Toys plc borrowed £15 000 to start business on 1 April. The line graph shows the financial balance each month. Copy and complete the table, using the information in the graph.

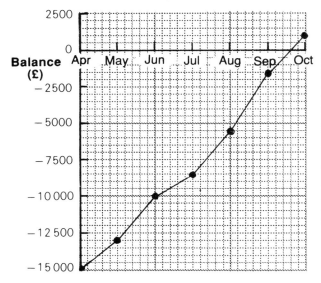

Date	Profit (£) for previous month	Balance (£)
1st April	—	−15 000
1st May	2000	−13 000
1st June		
1st July		
1st August		
1st September		
1st October		

EXERCISE 3F

Reminder

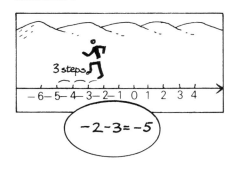

1 Calculate:

a $5+(-2)$	**b** $5-2$	**c** $8+(-3)$
d $2+(-6)$	**e** $4+(-4)$	**f** $3-5$
g $-3-1$	**h** $-1+(-5)$	**i** $8+(-8)$
j $-8+8$	**k** $2-9$	**l** $-1-1$
m $2x+(-x)$	**n** $y+(-2y)$	**o** $-3a-7a$
p $-b+(-b)$	**q** $-2c+(-5c)$	**r** $4d+(-d)$

2 Solve these equations:

a $x+(-5)=0$ **b** $x+(-1)=0$ **c** $x+(-3)=4$ **d** $x-2=-4$
e $x-1=-2$ **f** $x-7=-2$ **g** $x+(-1)=-1$ **h** $x+(-3)=-5$

3 Copy and complete the first three magic squares. The fourth one has a mistake in it for you to find.

a

−5		
−6	−4	
		−3

b

		−10
	−7	−5
		−6

c

−12	−10	−8
−7		

d

−3	2	−5
−4	3	0
1	−6	−1

4 Solve these equations:

    a $3-x=4$ **b** $-3-x=1$ **c** $-7-x=-5$

    d $4-x=-5$ **e** $5-x=10$ **f** $-3-x=-1$

5 Copy and complete these. For example, in **a** add then subtract, giving $-3+2-3=-4$ in the first line.

a   'Cross add off'

-3	2	3	-4
4	1	-2	7
	-3	-3	
-1		4	

b   'Cross off add'

-3	-2	1	0
		-3	17
	-3		
-8	-7		15

c   'Cross off off'

5	5	-2	2
		2	8
-4	-6		5
3			

6 Luigi is playing with a pack of cards. He imagines that the numbers on the red cards are positive and the numbers on the black cards are negative. He calls a set of three cards a *winner* if the cards can be arranged in order to make at least two correct subtractions.

 is a winner as it can be rearranged like this:  to give $-3-(-7)=4$,

and also like this:  to give $-3-4=-7$.

  a By rearranging these cards find as many winners as you can. In (i) you have the numbers -3, -1, -4; in (ii) -2, 6, 8 and so on.

(i) 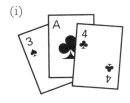   (ii) 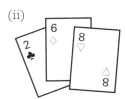   (iii) 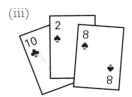   (iv)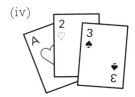

(v) 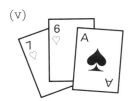   (vi) 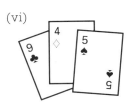   (vii) 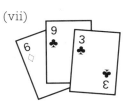   (viii)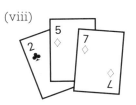

b Each set of cards below, in the order shown, makes a correct subtraction. Write down an equation for each, solve it and suggest two suitable cards for each hidden card. (*Hint* For (i), $3 - x = -4$.)

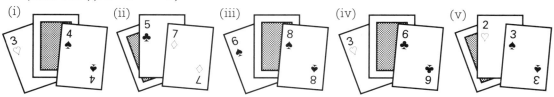

Brainstormer

Given $0°C = 32°F$ and $100°C = 212°F$, draw a straight line graph which can be used to convert all temperatures from $0°F$ to $250°F$ to corresponding temperatures in the Celsius scale. What are the Celsius equivalents of $0°F$ and $250°F$?

EXERCISE 4F

Islands— an Investigation

1 a Draw two circular islands and put a positive or negative number in each, for example 3 and 4.

b Join the islands by a 'halfway' island. In it enter the difference between the numbers in the first two islands $(3 - 4 = -1 \text{ or } 4 - 3 = 1)$.

c You now have three islands. Join any two of them, by marking in a halfway island and its difference number.

d Continue joining islands, making new 'difference' islands. The only rule is: When an island has three routes from it (for example '-1' in the diagram) it cannot be used again.

e Eventually there will be no usable islands left, for example:

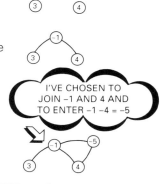

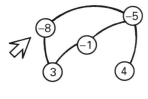 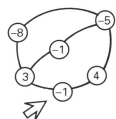 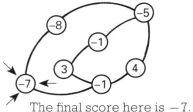

The final score here is -7.

2 a What is the smallest final score you can get with starting numbers 3 and 4?

b What is the largest score?   **c** How close can you get to zero?

d How are these answers related to the starting numbers?

3 Find out how the map grows and investigate the final scores obtained when you start with three islands.

4 Play this game with a partner. Start with three islands.

a Take turns to make new halfway islands.

b The person with the lowest total final score after five games is the winner.

8 ROUND IN CIRCLES

In calculations, take 3.14 for π or use the calculator π key. Round off your answers to three significant figures.

EXERCISE 1F

1  The 'rotor wire wheel' brush has a diameter of 14 cm. The hub in the centre has a radius of 3 cm. Calculate the width of the bristles on the brush.

2 **a** Each complete turn of the screw on the hose clip reduces the diameter of the clip by 0.8 mm. If the screw is given 5 turns, by how much is the diameter reduced: (i) in mm (ii) in cm?
   b The diameter of the clip is 4 cm. How many turns of the screw are needed to tighten the clip on a hose with diameter 3 cm?

3

Gauge no.	Diameter (mm)
1	5.5
2	4.5
3	3.6
4	2.8
5	2.1
6	1.5
7	1.0
8	0.6
9	0.3
10	0.1

The gauge is used for measuring the diameter of wire.
a Two wires have gauge numbers 5 and 9.
  Find the difference between their radii.
b Find the diameters and gauge numbers of two wires whose diameters differ by 1.7 mm, using the gauge.
c The radii of another pair of wires differ by 0.25 mm. Find their two possible pairs of gauge numbers.

4 **a** A circle with diameter 6 units passes through $(2, 2)$ and $(8, 2)$. Find the coordinates of its centre.
   b A circle with radius 4 units passes through $(-1, -3)$ and $(-1, 5)$. Find the coordinates of its centre.
   c A circle with radius 3 units passes through $(-2, 2)$ and $(1, -1)$. Can you find the coordinates of two possible points for its centre?
   d A circle passes through $(-3, -1)$ and $(6, 2)$. Try to find four possible points for its centre for each of which you can state the radius without having to measure it.

EXERCISE 2F

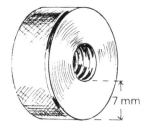

1 The radius of the hole in the ring is 3 mm. Calculate:
   a the diameter and circumference of the ring, in cm
   b the number of turns made by the ring in rolling down a 5 metre slope (to the nearest turn).

2

The 'Wall of Death' has a diameter of 80 m and 'The Silver Streak' circles on a motorbike at 20 m/s. Calculate:
   a the circumference of the wall
   b the number of circuits by the motorbike in 5 minutes
   c the speed of the bike to make 4 circuits per minute.

3 Janine uses this picture in her computer game. The radius of the arc is 12 mm.
   a What fraction of a full circle is the part from A to B?
   b Calculate the length of the dotted arc.

4 This dial gauge measures small movements in or out of the stem. When the stem is pushed in 1 mm the hand on the dial makes one complete turn.
   a The hand moves clockwise from 0 to 20. How far in is the stem pushed?
   b The stem is pushed in 5 mm. Calculate the distance travelled by the tip of the hand.
   c The tip of the hand moves 8 cm. Calculate the distance, to the nearest 0.1 mm, that the stem is pushed in.

5 A steel rod has a diameter of 16.0 ± 0.05 cm.
   a Write down the greatest and least values of the diameter.
   b In rolling 80 metres, how many more turns would the smallest size make compared to the largest?

Brainstormer
The centre of the small washer is level with the bottom of the hole in the larger washer.
   a Find the diameter of the small washer. Describe your reasoning.
   b The washers roll down a 5 m slope. The large one turns twice each second, the small one three times. Which arrives at the bottom of the slope first?

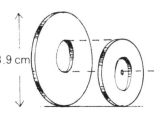

EXERCISE 3F

1 a

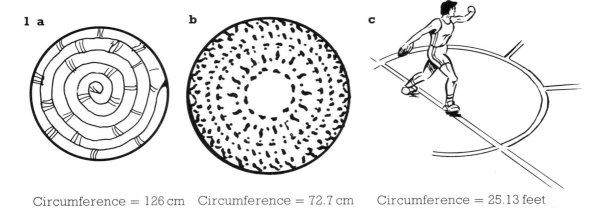

Circumference = 126 cm   Circumference = 72.7 cm   Circumference = 25.13 feet

Calculate the diameters of the circles above.

2 A ten-pin bowling ball rolls 18.3 m, turning 27 times, before it hits the first pin. Calculate the diameter of the ball in cm to 1 decimal place.

3 Edward is an enthusiast for old bicycles. He measures the circumference of the front wheel, 6 metres! He finds that the rear wheel makes 10 turns for every 3 turns of the front wheel. Calculate:
a the circumference   **b** the diameter, of the rear wheel.

4 Edward has to fit a new rear wheel. To find its circumference, he cycles for 12 turns of the front wheel.
a What distance does he travel?
b How many turns would his original rear wheel have made?
c The new one makes 4 turns less than the original one. Calculate its circumference.
d Calculate its radius.

5 In basketball the semicircle behind the 'free throw line' must be 565 cm long. Calculate, to the nearest centimetre, the radius of the semicircle.

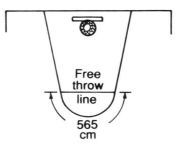

Free throw line

565 cm

EXERCISE 4F

1 Hole Saws can be used to cut washers out of sheet metal.

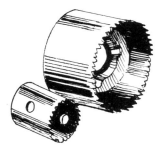

a Types HS 160 and HS 220 are used to cut out washers like the ones in the Brainstormer on page 38. Calculate the area of one of the flat sides of the washer.

Type	Cutting diameter (mm)
HS 160	16.0
HS 190	19.0
HS 205	20.5
HS 220	22.0

b Another washer has a flat surface area of 97 mm². Which two types of saw are used to cut it?

c A special washer is cut out using HS 600 and four holes are cut in it using HS 160, 190, 205 and 220. What is the area of one of its flat surfaces?

2

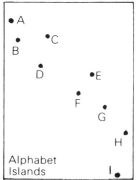

Calculate the area of:

a the hole in this lock nut

b metal on the flat surface of the nut.
(*Hint*   Sketch the nut, with six triangles in it.)

3 a A group of islands is struck by an earthquake centred on Island D. The circular danger-zone covers an area of 200 000 km².
Calculate: (i) the radius of the danger-zone
(ii) the number of islands in the danger-zone.

b A second shock, centred on another island, has a circular danger-zone of 80 000 km². If only two other islands are in this zone, which island is the epicentre of the quake now?

9 TYPES OF TRIANGLE

EXERCISE 1F

1 Make an equation for each triangle, solve it and write down the sizes of the angles.

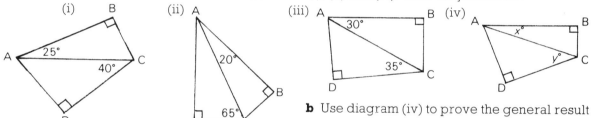

a $(2x+30)°$ $(3x-15)°$

b $5x°$ $(50-x)°$

c $(x+3)°$ $(8x+6)°$

d $x°$ $(80-y)°$ $(4x-10)°$ $3y°$

2 a Calculate the value of $\angle DAB + \angle DCB$ in (i), (ii) and (iii). What do you notice?

(i) B, A, 25°, 40°, C, D

(ii) A, 20°, 65°, D, C, B

(iii) A, 30°, B, 35°, D, C

(iv) A, $x°$, B, $y°$, C, D

b Use diagram (iv) to prove the general result you noticed.

3 Make an equation for each triangle, solve it and find the sizes of all of the angles

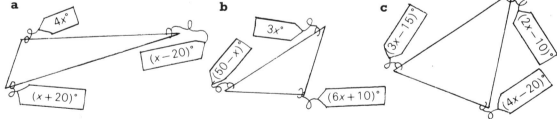

a $4x°$ $(x-20)°$ $(x+20)°$

b $3x°$ $(50-x)°$ $(6x+10)°$

c $(3x-15)°$ $(2x-10)°$ $(4x-20)°$

4 Lionel is puzzled. Which three labels should he choose, and for which angles?

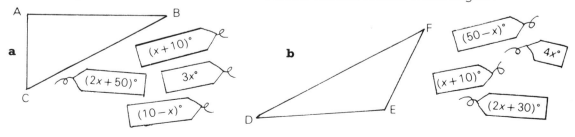

a A, B, C, $(x+10)°$, $(2x+50)°$, $3x°$, $(10-x)°$

b F, D, E, $(50-x)°$, $4x°$, $(x+10)°$, $(2x+30)°$

EXERCISE 2F

1 Find the areas of these triangles.

a

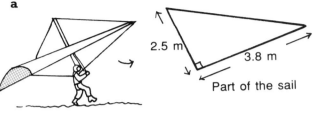

2.5 m
3.8 m
Part of the sail

Hang-glider

b

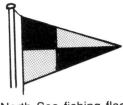

North Sea fishing flag

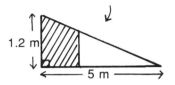

1.2 m
5 m

2 a Calculate the area of triangle ABC.

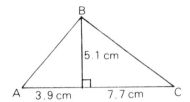

B
5.1 cm
A   3.9 cm   7.7 cm   C

b Find the length of PS.

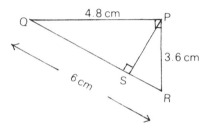

Q   4.8 cm   P
3.6 cm
6 cm   S
R

3 a Calculate the shortest distance from C to the footpath.

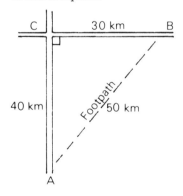

C   30 km   B
40 km   Footpath   50 km
A

b Arrange the areas of the four enclosures in order.

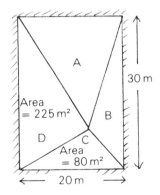

A
30 m
Area = 225 m²   B
D   C
Area = 80 m²
20 m

Brainstormer

A is the point (0, 1) and B is (3, 0). Placing C at (4, 3) gives triangle ABC an area of 5 squares. Check this.

Find four more positions of C with whole number coordinates which give ABC an area of 5 squares.

Investigate further, marking the areas given by C at different points to see the patterns.

EXERCISE 3F

1 Make an equation for each
isosceles triangle and
solve it to find the sizes of
all of the angles in the
triangles.

2

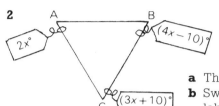

Lionel labelled the angles of this isosceles triangle.
$\angle A = \angle B$, so $2x = 4x - 10$, from which $x = 5$.

a This makes the angles 10°, 10° and 25°. Why will this not do?
b Swap $2x°$ and $(3x + 10)°$ and start again. Is this sensible
labelling?

3 These are sets of angles in isosceles triangles. Which is the odd one in each?
a $(4x - 5)°$, $(50 - x)°$, $(3x + 15)°$ **b** $3x°$, $(x - 10)°$, $(70 - x)°$.

4 A straw 74 cm long is cut into three pieces of lengths $2x$ cm, $2x$ cm and $3x + 4$ cm to form
an isosceles triangle. Make an equation and solve it to find the three lengths.

5 Repeat question **4** for lengths $2x$ cm, $x + 5$ cm and $3x - 4$ cm. There are three possible
lengths for the original straw.

6 The area of glass in the window is 2.16 m².
Calculate:
a the height of the window
b x, in cm
c y, in cm, and the height of pane A
d the area of: (i) pane A   (ii) pane B.

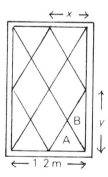

7

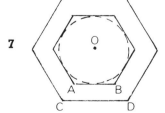

This is the cross-section of a box-spanner. The diameter of the
inside circle is 40 mm and the thickness of the spanner is 5 mm.
AB = 23.1 mm and CD = 28.9 mm. Find the area of the cross-
section of the spanner.
(*Hint*   Copy the diagram and draw OAC and OBD.)

EXERCISE 4F

Anwar invented a new puzzle. A clear plastic equilateral triangle
has to be fitted into its frame so that the dots, which show on both
sides of the plastic, match at each corner.
The triangle can be taken from the frame
and fitted back in six different ways:

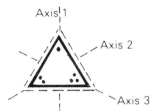

R_1 = rotate it 360° about the centre
R_2 = rotate it 120° clockwise about the centre
R_3 = rotate it 240° clockwise about the centre
F_1 = flip it about axis 1
F_2 = flip it about axis 2
F_3 = flip it about axis 3

1 If the triangle is fitted as shown in each diagram, which move will make its dots match
those in the frame?

a 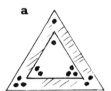   **b** 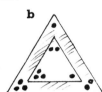   **c** 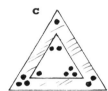   **d**   **e**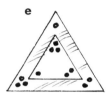

Anwar found that sometimes he could make two moves to make the dots fit.

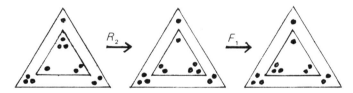

2 Copy and complete this table for all possible pairs of moves:

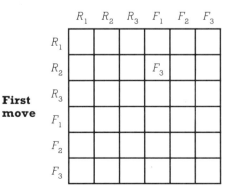

Second move

	R_1	R_2	R_3	F_1	F_2	F_3
R_1						
R_2			F_3			
R_3						
F_1						
F_2						
F_3						

First move (to the left of the rows R_1–F_3)

EXERCISE 5F

1 Calculate the sizes of the angles of these triangles:

a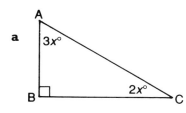

b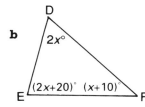

c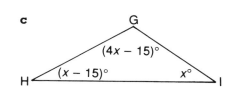

2 Which of these triangles is right-angled, isosceles, equilateral or scalene (all sides and angles unequal)?
   a △XYZ, with ∠XYZ = 42° and ∠YXZ = 38°.
   b △UVW, with ∠UVW = 60° and UV = WV = 8 cm.
   c △RST, with ∠RST = 37°, ∠RTS = 53°.
   d △OPQ, with ∠OPQ = 26°, ∠OQP = 128°.

3 Triangles KNM and HIJ are isosceles. Calculate the size of each angle.

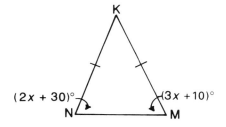

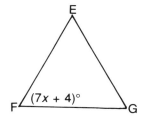

4 Triangle EFG is equilateral. Calculate the value of x.

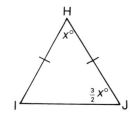

5

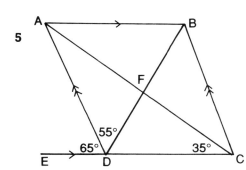

Copy the diagram and fill in the sizes of all the angles.

6 a Make an accurate drawing of the arrowhead.
   b Measure the size of the marked angle.

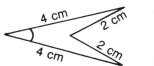

EXERCISE 6F

Use tracing paper for this exercise.

The police are using two detector vans to trace an illegal transmitter. They use a baseline and two angle readings to draw a triangle and pinpoint the transmitter (which moves around to avoid detection). Find the location for each of these reports. Assume that the vans are parked on the roads. Use the scale shown below the map.

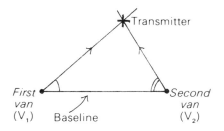

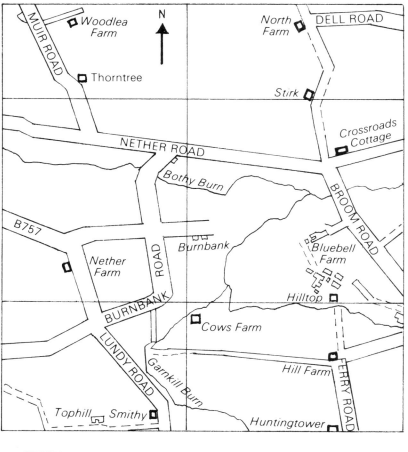

0   500   1000   1500 **Metres**

Scale:

1 April 13, 20 00 hours
   V_1 at junction of Muir Rd and Nether Rd; V_2 at Crossroads Cottage. Transmitter to the North.
   Angles: V_1 35°, V_2 68°

2 April 14, 23 30 hours
   V_1 at Nether Farm; V_2 at Smithy. Transmitter to the East.
   Angles: V_1 40°, V_2 103°

3 April 15, 18 15 hours
   V_1 at junction of Lundy Rd and Burnbank Rd; V_2 at Crossroads Cottage.
   Angles: V_1 59°, V_2 52°
   Find two possible locations, and their distances from each police van.

4 Make up similar questions, using the map or a street map of your own area. Challenge a friend to find the transmitter in each case.

EXERCISE 7F

1 a Calculate the number of dots in each of
the first ten patterns of this sequence:

b Why are these called **triangular
numbers**?

2 a Count the number of small 'right way
up' triangles ($\triangle$) in each pattern.
b How many are there in:
(i) the tenth pattern
(ii) the twentieth pattern?

c (i) Calculate the number of 'right way up' triangles *of all sizes* in each of the first six
patterns. (Be methodical—number of triangles in each pattern with sides of length
1 unit, 2 units, . . .)
(ii) How many triangles are there in the twentieth pattern?

3 a Calculate the number of triangles of all sizes in the first six patterns of this sequence.
How are these numbers connected with triangular numbers?
b How many triangles are there in the tenth pattern?

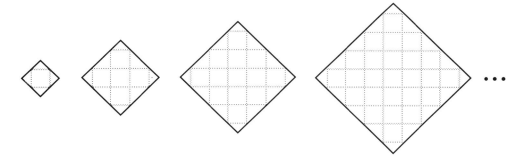

4 Solve this cross-number puzzle. The clues are based on the sequence of triangular
numbers 1, 3, 6, 10, ... $T_1 = 1$, $T_2 = 3$, $T_3 = 6$, and so on.

Clues Across

2   T_{17}
4   $T_6 + T_8$
5   $T_{11} - T_2$
7   T_7
8   $T_3 \times T_3 + T_3$
9   $4T_6$
11 $T_2 \times T_2 \times T_2 + \frac{1}{2}T_8$
12 $5T_{14}$

Clues Down

1   T_5
2   $3T_8 - T_{13}$
3   $T_5 + T_5$
4   $T_6 \times T_7$
6   $T_{14} + 2T_{15}$
10 $T_{16} - T_{13}$
11 T_9
13 $T_1 + T_2 + T_3 + T_4$

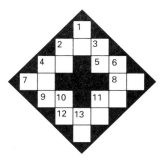

10 METRIC MEASURE

EXERCISE 1F

1 Calculate the perimeters of these shapes:

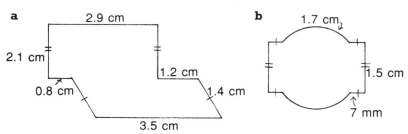

a 2.9 cm, 2.1 cm, 0.8 cm, 1.2 cm, 1.4 cm, 3.5 cm

b 1.7 cm, 1.5 cm, 7 mm

2 Taking 1 km to be nearly 0.625 mile, convert the speed limits of 100 km/h, 60 km/h and 45 km/h to the nearest number of miles per hour.

3 a Calculate the distance right around this 'tourist triangle' in London.
   b How much shorter is the direct route from the British Museum to Buckingham Palace than the route via the Houses of Parliament?

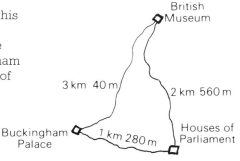

British Museum
3 km 40 m
2 km 560 m
Buckingham Palace
1 km 280 m
Houses of Parliament

4 A motorway 9.7 km long is being extended by 1800 m. Find its new length:
   a in kilometres   **b** in metres.

5 Calculate in metres the total length of wire needed to make each of these regular skeleton models:

a 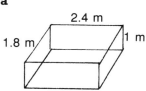 2.4 m, 1.8 m, 1 m

b  17.5 cm

c 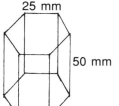 25 mm, 50 mm

d 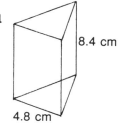 8.4 cm, 4.8 cm

6 Thirty lamp-posts are evenly spaced in a straight line, thirty-five metres apart. Calculate the distance in km between the first and last lamp-post.

7 A roll of wallpaper is 10.05 m long. The height of a wall to be papered is 2.3 m. How many strips can be cut from the roll if:
a no matching of patterns is necessary
b 25 cm have to be allowed in each strip for matching patterns?
How much of the roll remains in each case?

Investigation

Sports pitches have to be marked out at Newton High School playing fields; they are a rugby pitch (100 m by 60 m), a football pitch (90 m by 50 m) and two hockey pitches (each 80 m by 50 m). A minimum of 10 m has to be left between pitches and the school, between the pitches themselves and between the pitches and the perimeter fence.

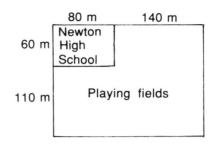

Investigate possible placing of the pitches and make scale drawings in which 1 cm represents 20 m. Label your drawings clearly.

EXERCISE 2F

> *Reminder*
> $1 \text{ cm}^2 = 100 \text{ mm}^2$
> $1 \text{ m}^2 = 10\,000 \text{ cm}^2$
> $1 \text{ hectare} = 10\,000 \text{ m}^2$

1 Calculate the shaded areas. All the angles are right angles.

a
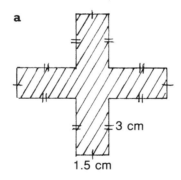

b
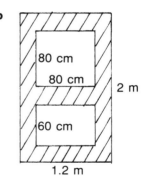

2 A roll of ribbon is 8 m long and 8 mm wide. Calculate the area of one surface of the ribbon.

3 Farmer Jones buys 1 hectare of land. On it he builds two barns, one 40 m by 30 m, the other 50 m by 35 m. What area of land is left?

4 What is the least number of rectangular tiles 24 cm by 16 cm needed to cover a floor 6 m long and 4 m wide?

5 Calculate the number of hectares in 1 square kilometre.

6 This lounge floor has to be covered with pine planks, each 2 m long and 10 cm wide. How many planks should be ordered?

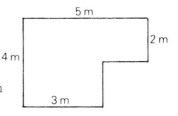

7

65 x 3-PLY TISSUES
SHEET SIZE 300 mm x 276 mm
TOTAL AREA 5.38 sq metres

This notice appears on boxes of tissues sold in a High Street Store. Is their calculation correct? Think carefully about your answer.

8 Here is a plan of the new 9-hole Bluesky Golf Course. The lengths are in metres. Calculate:
   a the length of the course
      (i) in m   (ii) in km
   b the mean length of a hole, to the nearest metre
   c the approximate area in hectares taken up by the course.

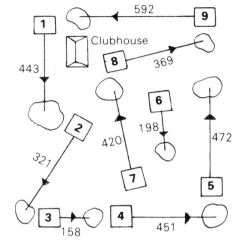

9 Mr Patel has made a new garden fence. It has 18 panels and supporting posts. Each panel is 1.8 m long and 1.2 m high and each post measures 2 m by 10 cm by 10 cm. How many tins of preservative will he have to buy for both sides of the fence, including posts, if one tin covers 25 m²?

10 A warehouse has a rectangular floor space 29 m by 18 m. Crates measuring 2.5 m by 2.4 m by 90 cm have to be stored, but one cannot be put on top of another. What is the maximum number of crates that can be stored?

EXERCISE 3F

Reminder
1 litre = 1000 ml
    = 1000 cm³
1 litre = 100 centilitres

1 Calculate the volumes of these solids made of cuboids:

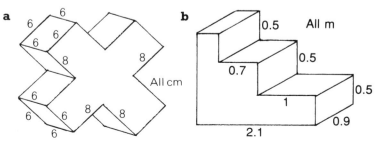

2 A carton of fruit juice is in the shape of a cuboid with base 10 cm by 6 cm.
   a What will the height of the carton have to be so that it holds 1 litre of juice and has an air space of 20 cm³?
   b How many glasses of juice, each holding 150 ml, can be filled from the carton?

3 Calculate the volume in cm³ of a wooden shelf 3 m long, 20 cm broad and 7 mm thick.

4 How many litres of water are needed to make a skating rink 25 m long, 20 m wide and 30 mm thick?

5 An oil storage tank in the shape of a cuboid has dimensions 2.5 m by 2 m by 1 m. How long does it take to fill at 160 litres per minute?

6 a Calculate the volume of this swimming pool: (i) in m³   (ii) in litres.
   b Find the depth of water, to the nearest cm, in the shallow end when the pool is three quarters full.

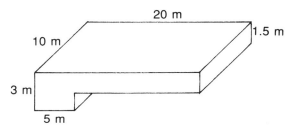

7 Speedie and Co. have a van with a load-carrying space 4.3 m long, 1.5 m wide and 1.9 m high.
   a How many 2 m by 12 cm by 12 cm posts can be carried in it?
   b How many smaller posts 1.8 m by 12 cm by 12 cm can be put in the remaining space?

EXERCISE 4F

> *Reminder*
> 1000 mg = 1 g
> 1000 g   = 1 kg
> 1000 kg = 1 tonne

1 Twelve tonnes of gravel chips have to be transported on a trailer which can take a maximum load of 1800 kg. How many trips will be necessary?

2 A cardboard box weighs 350 g. When filled with 24 cans of cola it weighs 11.15 kg. Calculate the weight of a can of cola: **a** in kilograms.   **b** in grams.

3 Simon saves 50p coins. He has £97.50 worth of them, weighing 2 kg 633 g. Calculate the weight of: **a** a 50p coin, to the nearest tenth of a gram
   b £100 worth of 50p coins, in kg.

4 Enid the elephant weighs 1.76 tonnes, Clarence the cat 2.9 kg, Michèle the mouse 80 g and Philip the fly 160 mg. How many times heavier, to the nearest whole number, is:
   a Michèle than Philip   **b** Clarence than Michèle and Philip together
   c Enid than Clarence, Michèle and Philip together?

5 Supersize packs of teabags hold 750 teabags and weigh $2\frac{1}{4}$ kg. Find the weight of one teabag.

6 Airmail rates in 1993 were:

Rates from UK to:		Up to 10 g	Up to 20 g	Up to 40 g	Each extra 20 g (or part of 20 g) add:
Europe:	EC	24p	24p	39p	11p
	non EC	28p	28p	39p	11p
Australasia, Japan, China		39p	57p	99p	42p
Elsewhere		39p	57p	89p	32p

Calculate the total cost of six letters to pen-pals in:
New York 18 g, Tokyo 15 g, Sydney 27 g, Delhi 8 g, Cairo 40 g, Quebec 62 g.

7 The Silver Steel Company make a series of similar solid steel cuboids. The two smallest sizes are shown. The smaller one weighs 1.5 kg.

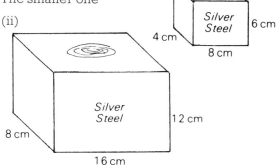

  a Calculate the volume of each cuboid.
  b What is the weight of the second one?
  c The next one they make is 24 cm high. What are its length, breadth and weight?
  d What are the length, breadth, height and weight of the fourth cuboid?
  e A special order is for a 32 cm by 24 cm by 8 cm cuboid. How much would it weigh?
  f Find as many whole number lengths, breadths and heights as possible for a steel cuboid weighing 1.5 kg.

11 EQUATIONS AND INEQUATIONS

EXERCISE 1F

1 For each set of straws make an equation, solve it and write down the lengths of all the straws. Lengths are in cm.

a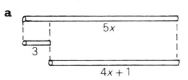

b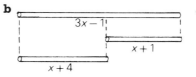

c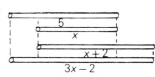

d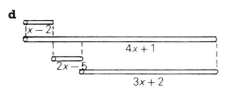

e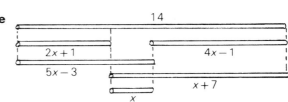

2 Alma and Alfred make a wire trellis from a 60 m roll of wire. They lay lengths of wire across each other to form a grid of squares as shown.

a The shorter wires are x m long. What length are the longer wires, in terms of x?

b Make an equation and solve it to find the two different lengths of wire to the nearest possible cm.

c What length of wire is left over on the roll?

d They bind every intersection on the grid with thin wire from a 10 m roll. What length of wire, to the nearest cm, can they use for each join?

e Alma and Alfred become more ambitious and decide to make a trellis of equilateral triangles. They want the side of each triangle to be 50–60 cm long. To calculate the size of trellis they can make with 60 m of wire, they start with one small triangle, then four and so on. What length should they make each side and how much wire will they have left over?

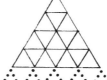

3 sides

9 sides

3 Starting with two equal straws, one is cut into two pieces. The three lengths (in cm) are given. In each question, form a suitable equation and solve it to find the three lengths.

a

$$x + 7$$
$$3x + 1$$
$$4x$$

b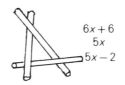

$$6x + 6$$
$$5x$$
$$5x - 2$$

c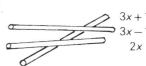

$$3x + 1$$
$$3x - 1$$
$$2x$$

d

$$3x - 4$$
$$2x + 2$$
$$x - 2$$

e

$$3x + 2$$
$$x$$
$$2x + 3$$

(Lengths need not be whole numbers)

f

$$4x$$
$$8 - x$$
$$2x + 1$$

(Two possibilities)

g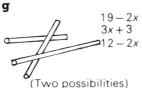

$$19 - 2x$$
$$3x + 3$$
$$12 - 2x$$

(Two possibilities)

h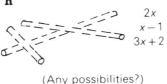

$$2x$$
$$x - 1$$
$$3x + 2$$

(Any possibilities?)

i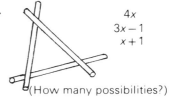

$$4x$$
$$3x - 1$$
$$x + 1$$

(How many possibilities?)

4 Starting again with two equal straws, one *or both* are cut into pieces. Find the four lengths and the length of the original straws (two sets in each case).

a

$$2x$$
$$x - 1$$
$$2x - 2$$
$$3x - 5$$

b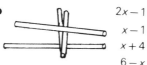

$$2x - 1$$
$$x - 1$$
$$x + 4$$
$$6 - x$$

c

$$x + 5$$
$$2x - 1$$
$$2x$$
$$4 - x$$

Brainstormers

1 Two straws of equal length are cut, one into three pieces and the other into two pieces. The lengths of the pieces are $4x$, $3x + 2$, $x + 6$, x and x cm. Find two possible lengths for the original straws.

2 Two equal straws are cut into a total of five pieces of lengths x, x, $2x$, $x + 1$ and $3 - x$ cm. Find four different sets of lengths for the pieces and the straws.

EXERCISE 2F

1 Solve these equations:

a $2x = x + 1$
b $3(x + 1) = 4x$
c $6x = 5(x + 2)$
d $4x + 1 = 3(x + 1)$
e $4(x - 1) = 5x - 11$
f $2(x + 1) = 3(x - 3)$
g $3(x - 1) = 4(x - 2)$
h $2(x - 1) + 5x = 8(x - 1)$
i $5x + x(x - 2) = x(x + 6) - 9$
j $3(3 + x) = 2(x + 7)$
k $5(2 - 2x) + 12x = 4(10 - x)$

2 For **a**, **b**, **c** and **d** find: (i) the perimeter   (ii) the area, in terms of x, of each rectangle. Then, use these expressions to answer (iii) and (iv). (All figures are rectangles.)

a

8 cm

2x + 3 cm

(iii) If perimeter = 30 cm, find the area.
(iv) If area = 40 cm², find the perimeter.

b

3x - 2 cm

10 cm

(iii) If perimeter = 46 cm, find the area.
(iv) If area = 190 cm², find the perimeter.

c

18 mm

x - 5 mm

(iii) If perimeter = 4x mm, find the area.
(iv) If area = 8x mm², find the perimeter.

d

2x + 1 m

7 m

(iii) If perimeter = 2(3x − 1) m, find the area.
(iv) If area = 3(x + 28) m², find the perimeter.

3 Rope tricks!

a 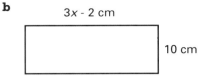 $4x$ metres of rope are used to fence this rectangular enclosure.

← 5 m →

(i) Explain why the width of the enclosure is $2x - 5$ metres.
(ii) Find an expression, in terms of x, for the area enclosed.
(iii) The area enclosed is 15 m². Make an equation and solve it to find the length of the rope.

b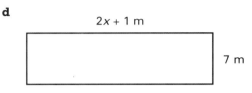

$6x$ metres are used to enclose this area:

Area = 20m²   ↕ 4 m

How long is the rope?

c

$2x$ metres are used to enclose this area:

Area = 5x m² ↕ 10 m

How long is the rope?

d

$8x$ metres are used to enclose this area:

5 m

This distance is **4 metres.**

The area enclosed is $6x$ m². What is the length of the rope?

EXERCISE 3F

On the airlines

Write inequations for these:

1

PASSENGERS ARE ALLOWED
NO MORE THAN 30kg OF
BAGGAGE FREE. ANY MORE
THAN THIS WILL BE CHARGED
AN EXCESS FEE.

   a Anne O'Brian, with x kg baggage, was not charged.
   b Bob Milne, with y kg baggage, was charged an excess fee.

2 **a** Mr Arbuckle received a full refund when he cancelled x days before his flight.
   b Mrs Donlevy did not receive a full refund y days before her flight.

FULL REFUND OF FARE WILL BE
GIVEN IF CANCELLATION IS AT LEAST
14 DAYS IN ADVANCE OF FLIGHT.

3

DRY-ICE IN QUANTITIES
NOT EXCEEDING 2kg MAY
BE CARRIED ON THE PLANE.

   a Mrs Reid was not allowed t kg of dry-ice onto the plane.
   b Mr Abbishaw was allowed on with his w kg of dry-ice packing his perishables.

4 **a** At the airport, x year old Abbi paid 50% of normal fare.
   b Her sister Anni y years old, only paid 10% of normal fare.

INFANTS UNDER 2 YEARS OLD
PAY 10% OF NORMAL FARE.

5 Students aged 12–26 years, inclusive, are granted a 25% discount. Ewan, aged y years, is a student who got this discount.

6 Children 2 years of age or more, but under 12 years, are entitled to a 50% reduction on normal fare; x years old Rosie got this reduction and paid £y. The normal fare was more than £320, but not more than £400.

12 RATIO AND PROPORTION

EXERCISE 1F

1 The recipes for these cakes include sugar and flour:

Type of cake	Weight in ounces of:		
	Whole cake	Sugar	Flour
Buttercake	18	2	9
Shortbread	12	3	4
Sponge	21	3	7
Cherry	28	$3\frac{1}{2}$	7

a (i) Find the ratio 'weight of sugar:weight of whole cake' in the form 1:... for each cake.

(ii) Arrange the cakes in order, with the smallest ratio of sugar to cake first.

b Repeat part **a** for 'weight of flour:weight of whole cake' for each cake.

2 Simon was 20 when his nephew Neil was born.
   a Calculate 'Neil's age:Simon's age' when Neil was: (i) 1   (ii) 5   (iii) 10 years old.
   b Repeat the calculations for a period of 50 years at 5 year intervals, giving each ratio in the form 1:... (to 2 decimal places where necessary).
   c Describe what happens to the ratios. (Include impossibly old people.)

Many machines with gears, crankshafts, levers and such like, involve calculations with ratios.
This lever will balance if
weight A:weight B = distance b:distance a.

(Notice that the heavier weight has to be nearer the point of balance than the smaller weight—as on a seesaw.)

3 a This lever is balanced

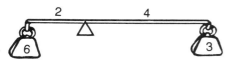

b This lever is not balanced

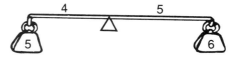

Calculate ratios of weights and distances to show that each of the statements above is true.

4 By calculating ratios of weights and distances, find which of these levers are balanced.

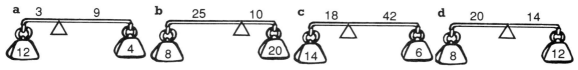

5 What weight has to be added, and if so, to which side, to make each lever balance?

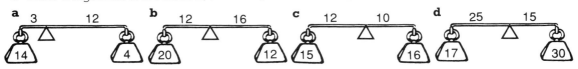

6 Where would you put the point of balance to keep each lever horizontal?

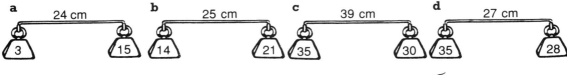

7 This balance is being kept horizontal. Which side will go down when the hand is taken away? Explain your answer.

EXERCISE 2F

---

1 Use the fact that these ratios are equal to find the missing numbers.

   a $2:1 = 6:\boxed{?}$ **b** $1:3 = 4:\boxed{?}$ **c** $1:6 = 4:\boxed{?}$

   d $1:5 = \boxed{?}:10$ **e** $3:4 = 6:\boxed{?}$ **f** $4:5 = \boxed{?}:20$

2 Chemically, coal falls into three types according to the ratio carbon:hydrogen:nitrogen:oxygen in a sample of the coal.

Type of coal	C : H : N : O
Lignite	1·: 7 : 2 : 28
Bituminous	1 : 7 : 2 : 10
Anthracite	1 : 3 : 1 : 3

   a What weight of carbon content would you expect in 1520 tonnes of:
     (i) lignite   (ii) bituminous
   (iii) anthracite?
   b A sample has a nitrogen content of 10 g. What oxygen content would you expect to find if the sample is: (i) lignite   (ii) bituminous   (iii) anthracite?
   c A sample has a hydrogen content of 21 g. What other information, if any, do you need to identify the coal type if the nitrogen content is: (i) 6 g   (ii) 7 g?

3 Richard, Rachael and Scott booked a set meal and paid in advance, £4.50, £9 and £6 respectively. On the night they found that they had to pay £5.20 more on the total bill.
   a How much extra had each to pay, keeping to the ratio of the advance payments?
   b How much would they have each got back if £1.30 had been overpaid?

4 In the Hall of Mirrors the mirrors distort everything. One mirror enlarges height in the ratio 3:1 and width in the ratio 2:1.
   a A 4 cm by 2 cm rectangle is reflected in the mirror. Calculate the height and width of its image when the rectangle is held: (i) crossways   (ii) up and down.

  b Find the ratio 'area of image:area of original rectangle'.

  c What is the ratio 'height:width of a rectangle' whose image is a square?

  d Repeat **a**, **b** and **c** for mirrors which enlarge:
    (i) height 4:1 and width 3:1   (ii) height 3:2 and width 2:1.

  e If the height is increased in the ratio $x:1$ and the breadth in the ratio $y:1$, find:
    (i) the ratio 'area of image:area of original rectangle'
    (ii) the dimensions of a rectangle which turns into a square.

EXERCISE 3F

In 1989 the Post Office issued a set of four stamps for the anniversary of the Royal Microscopical Society.

   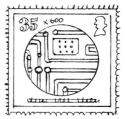

The 19p stamp shows a snowflake, 10 times actual size (× 10, scale 10:1).
The other stamps show a blue fly (× 5), blood cells (× 500) and a microchip (× 600).

1 Express the scales for the blue fly, blood cells and microchip as ratios . . . :1.

2 Some real lengths are:
  a a leaf on the snowflake, 0.5 mm
  b the head of the fly, 1.8 mm
  c a column of cells, 0.02 mm
  d a rectangle on the chip, 0.015 mm × 0.012 mm.
  What are their sizes on the stamps?

3 Some measurements from the stamps are:
  a a branch on the snowflake, 13 mm
  b a leg on the fly, 15 mm
  c a red blood cell, 2 mm
  d a microchip junction, 3 mm.
  Calculate the actual length of each part.

4 A stamp catalogue illustrates all four stamps at $\frac{3}{4}$ size.
  a Find the ratio 'length of snowflake in catalogue:actual length of snowflake'.
  b Repeat part **a** for the blue fly, blood cells and microchip.

5 Calculate the ratios of areas instead of lengths in question **4**.

6 a Terri wishes to have one of her holiday snaps enlarged and framed. Which of these frames will be suitable if the original photograph measures 130 mm by 100 mm?

   b The prices of the frames increase in the same ratio as the inner rectangular areas. Frame A costs 60p. How much is:
   (i) Frame B
   (ii) Frame F?

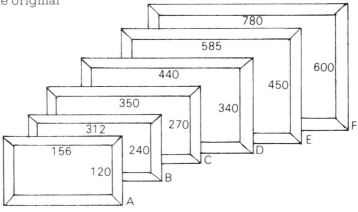

EXERCISE 4F

1 a Tina the trapeze artiste is 120 cm tall. One morning her shadow is 100 cm long and her dad's shadow is 150 cm long. How tall is her dad?

   b If she stood on her father's head, what would be the length of their shadow?

   c Some hours later, Tina's shadow was 150 cm long. What length was her dad's shadow then?

2 Calculating the impossible!

   a A pile of three 5p coins is 5 mm in height. What height is a pile which is worth £1?

   b A pile of 5p coins stretches from the Earth to the Moon, 380 000 km distant. How much is the pile worth?

3 The cost of transport is directly proportional to the distance transported; 8 tonnes can be carried 40 kilometres for £10.

   a How much would it cost to transport the same load 72 kilometres?

   b If the bill for transporting the 8 tonnes came to £55, how far was it transported?

   c What would be a fair price to transport:
   (i)   4 tonnes   100 kilometres
   (ii) 12 tonnes   90 kilometres?

4 Jack was finding the depth of wells. He knew that the distance fallen was directly proportional to the *square* of the time taken to fall. In experiments he found that in 1 second a stone will fall 490 cm.
   Show that it will fall: **a** 19.6 m in 2 seconds   **b** 44.1 m in 3 seconds.

5 The weight which can be supported by a rope is directly proportional to the *square* of the thickness of the rope. A certain material used to make ropes is 3 cm thick and it can be used to lift 135 kg.

   a What weight could be borne by a rope 2 cm thick of the same material?

   b How thick would a rope need to be to bear a maximum of 2.4 kg?

EXERCISE 5F

Use this conversion graph to estimate answers.

1 Convert:
  a 2 Irish punts to £
  b £1.80 to US dollars
  c 1.60 Maltese pounds to
     Cypriot pounds.

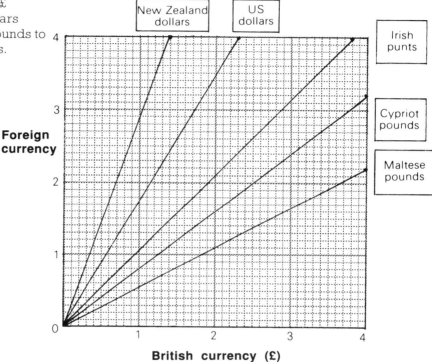

2 Convert:
  a £400 to Maltese pounds
  b 320 New Zealand
     dollars to £
  c 40 US dollars to New
     Zealand dollars.

3 Vic Masters received 629.20 Australian dollars for his £286. Between which two lines on the graph would you draw the Australian dollar line?

4 Make a conversion graph for these exchange rates for £1:
   Japan 264 yen, Spain 174 pesetas, Greece 276 drachmas, Portugal 251 escudos. You will have to plan the scales on the axes very carefully.

Investigation

Other topics can be illustrated by similar graphs, for example, miles travelled against petrol used for different makes of car. Investigate and illustrate such a topic.

EXERCISE 6F

Antonia is making a one-string lyre. The 50 cm string is tuned to middle C, with a frequency of 261.6 Hz. She knows the frequencies of the notes of the scale, as shown in the table.

She knows also that the frequency of a note is inversely proportional to the length of a vibrating string. She uses this to calculate that the fret for note 'A' should be positioned so as to allow 29.7 cm of string to vibrate.

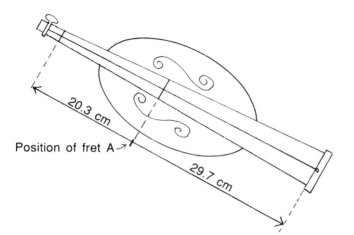

Note	Frequency
C	261.6
D	294.0
E	330.0
F	349.0
G	392.0
A	440.0
B	494.0
C'	523.2

1 Check Antonia's calculation for the position of fret A. Use the frequencies of 261.6 for note C and 440 for A.

2 Calculate the positions of the frets for the other six notes in the table.

Practical
Set up an experiment with a tin lid and a long elastic band to check that the frequency of a note *is* inversely proportional to the length of the band. A tuning fork will give you a starting note.

EXERCISE 7F

1 Two cubical containers have edges 3 m and 2 m long. Find the ratio, in the form $n:1$ of:
   a the lengths of their edges   **b** their surface areas   **c** their volumes.

2 A model aircraft is 12 cm long. The actual length of the aircraft is 8.64 m. The wing span of the model is 8.5 cm. What is the actual wing span?

3 £1 sterling is worth 2.75 marks.
   a What is the value, in marks, of £48?   **b** What is the value, in £s, of 220 marks?

4 At 45 rpm, a record plays for 12 minutes. How long would it play at $33\frac{1}{3}$ rpm?

5 A photographic slide measures 15 mm by 12 mm. The height of an image on a screen is 1 metre. What are the possible widths of the image?

6 The scale of a map is 1:200 000.
   a If two towns are 64 km apart, how far apart are they on the map?
   b Two other places are 4.3 cm apart on the map. What is the actual distance between them?

7 A builder contracts to complete some work in 48 days, using 14 people. After 16 days the work is held up by bad weather for 11 days. How many extra people are now needed to finish the work on time?

8 There are 204 Ordnance Survey maps of Britain which cover the 93 000 square miles of country. The area of the Earth's surface is 197 000 000 square miles, two-fifths of which is land. How many maps would be needed to cover all the land on Earth?

9 The spiral staircase to Australia has a large number of steps. It descends 6350 km and then ascends 6350 km. Nick counts 2500 steps as he descends 500 m.

   a How many steps are there in the staircase?
   b Each step is set at $22\frac{1}{2}°$ to the one above it. How many complete turns will Nick make on the whole staircase?

Investigation
The largest known prime number is $2^{756839} - 1$. When written out in full, this number has 227 832 digits. Investigate the number of lines and pages you would need in order to write out the number and the length of time the task would require.

13 MAKING SENSE OF STATISTICS 2

EXERCISE 1F

1 The table shows the number of hours that a group of students watched television one weekend.

No. of hours viewing	2	3	4	5	6	7
Frequency	3	5	7	9	10	7

a Find the mean, median and modal number of hours.
b Jim watched TV for 5 hours. Compare this with the rest of the group, using the averages and the range.

2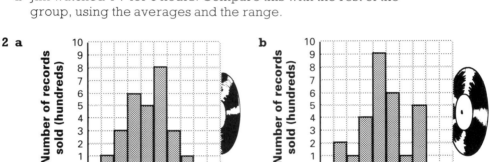

Forever   *Hear Me*

The frequency diagrams show the sales of two songs in the course of a week. Find the mean number of sales per day for each record.

3 A soap powder manufacturer launched a new improved version of their brand 'Supersuds.' They monitored the sales of both old and new brands over the next six months.

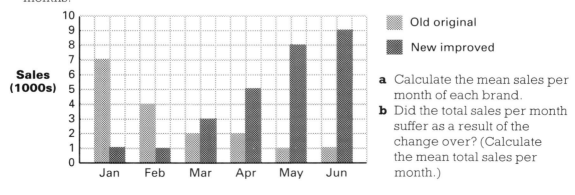

Old original

New improved

a Calculate the mean sales per month of each brand.
b Did the total sales per month suffer as a result of the change over? (Calculate the mean total sales per month.)

EXERCISE 2F

1 The lengths of TV programmes lasting less than 1 hour one day were noted.

No. of minutes	1–9	10–19	20–29	30–39	40–49	50–59
Frequency	1	5	6	9	4	5

   a Draw a frequency diagram of the results.
   b On the same diagram construct a frequency polygon.
   c What is the modal class?
   d What fraction of the programmes lasted 40 minutes or longer?

2 The frequency polygon shows how long a variety of seeds took to germinate in an experiment.
   a What is the range of germination times?
   b What is the most common length of time for a seed to germinate?
   c What is the mean germination time? (Take 5 to represent the class 1–10, and so on.)
   d What fraction of the seeds took longer than 50 hours to germinate?

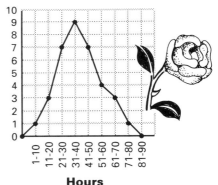

3 The frequency diagram illustrates the lengths of the vehicles aboard a ferry. The class interval includes the lower figure but not the upper.
   a Show the data in a table.
   b Calculate the mean and the modal lengths, using the mid-value of the class to represent the whole class.
   c Construct a frequency polygon.
   d (i) What fraction of the vehicles were 3.5 m or over?
   (ii) In 1000 vehicles, how many would you expect to be 3.5 m or over if they conform to the same pattern?

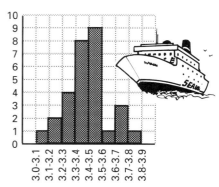
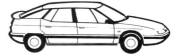

EXERCISE 3F

1 A survey was made of the ages of residents in the High Street.
The data was arranged in class intervals 0–10, 10–20 and so on.
The class 10–20 includes 10 year olds but not 20 year olds and can be represented by a mid-value of 15 years.
Use this information to copy and complete the table, and hence to calculate the mean age of residents in the High Street.

Age	Mid-value (M)	Frequency (F)	M × F
0–10	5	8	40
10–20	15	9	
20–30		12	
30–40		24	
40–50		15	
50–60		10	
60–70		7	

2 A survey of part of the sky known as 'Canis Major' was made and the magnitude of each star was noted (1 is brightest, 6 is dimmest).
The table shows a summary of the readings, to the nearest half magnitude.

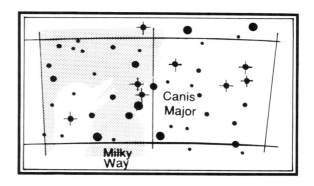

Magnitude	Frequency
1–1.5	2
2–2.5	3
3–3.5	4
4–4.5	12
5–5.5	20
6–6.5	58

Use the table to calculate the mean magnitude of stars in 'Canis Major'.

3 Politicians are very interested in the inflation rate of prices.

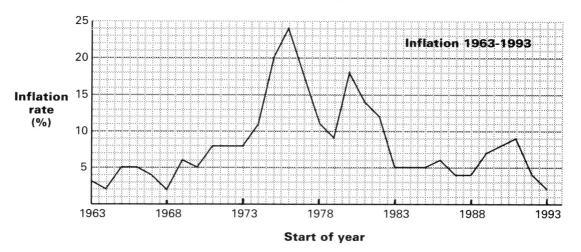

a Use the graph to help you to copy and complete the table.

Inflation rate (to nearest 0.1%)	Tally	Number of years with this rate
0–4.9		
5–9.9		
10–14.9		
15–19.9		
20–24.9		

b Calculate the mean rate of inflation over this period.

EXERCISE 4F

1 Here is a more accurate way of getting the
   line of best fit in a scatter diagram.
   This scatter diagram shows the Maths and
   Physics results (out of 10) in a class test.
   Each dot represents a different pupil.

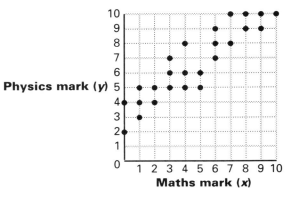

   a Make a list of the results as a set of
      coordinates $(0, 2)$, $(0, 4)$, $(1, 3)$, ...
   b Calculate the mean Maths mark and the
      mean Physics mark, and plot the mean
      point on a tracing, using O.

   c This splits the diagram
      into two parts:
      to the left of the mean
      (shaded) and to the
      right of the mean
      (unshaded)
      (i) Find the **mean
         point** of the shaded
         set and mark it with
         O.
      (ii) Repeat the process
         for the unshaded set.

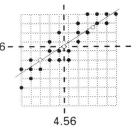

   d Draw the best fitting
      line through the
      three mean points.
      This line helps
      you predict
      values of y
      from values of x.

2 Use the above technique to get a best-fitting straight line which you can use to find the
   value of y in each case when x equals:
   (i) 3   (ii) 5   (iii) 7.

a
   The cost of a taxi
   journey depends on the
   length of the journey.

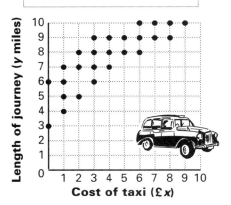

b
   A student's mark for effort
   will depend to some extent
   on attendance at school.

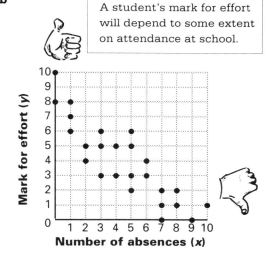

14 KINDS OF QUADRILATERAL

EXERCISE 1F

1 **a** The kite kit contains:
   (i) 8 rods with lengths of 30 cm, 40 cm, 50 cm, 72 cm and 78 cm.
   The total length of the rods is 428 cm.
   How many rods of each length are in the kit?
   (ii) 3-way joints  and 4-way joints ┼ . How many are there of each?

   b Sketch the kite and then make a scale drawing.
   c What area of fabric is needed for the kite?

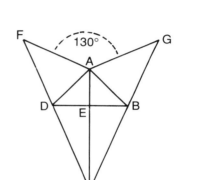

2 The diagram contains the kites ABCD, AEDF and AGBE.
   AEC is a line of symmetry.
   FDC and GBC are straight lines.
   a Sketch the diagram, showing the sizes of all the angles.
   b What shape is FCGA? How do you know?

3 O is the origin, A is (5, 2) and B(5, 5). Kite OABC has axis of symmetry OB.
   a Find the coordinates of C.
   b Under reflection in the *y*-axis, the image of OABC is ODEF. Write down the coordinates of this kite's vertices.
   c Complete the diagram so that it is symmetrical about the *x*-axis and write down the coordinates of all its other vertices.

EXERCISE 2F

1 PQRS is a rhombus.
   Copy it, and write in the sizes of all the angles.

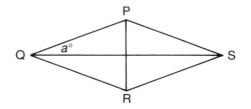

2 The star was obtained by drawing nine congruent rhombuses of side 5 cm round a point. Two sides of each rhombus were then erased.

   a Calculate the sizes of the angles of the rhombus.

   b On plain paper draw the nine angles at the centre using a protractor and a pencil.

   c Draw the star. You will need a ruler, compasses and an eraser.

3 An electric locomotive picks up power from the overhead wire through a vertical rhombus pantograph. Each side of the rhombus is 1 metre long. As the top of the rhombus rises and falls with the wire, the height of the rhombus can vary from 1.2 m to 1.6 m.

By means of scale drawings, find the maximum and minimum horizontal lengths of the rhombus.

EXERCISE 3F

1 Draw a line XY, 8 cm long. Using only compasses and a straight edge, bisect the line AB.

2 On plain paper draw a rectangle whose length is twice its breadth, using compasses and a straight edge only—no measuring with a ruler allowed!

3 Draw a large triangle ABC. Bisect each angle. Do you find that the three lines bisecting the angles meet at the same point?

4 a Using ruler and compasses only, construct an angle of 60°.

   b In this angle, construct angles of 30°, 15° and $7\frac{1}{2}$°.

EXERCISE 4F

Wallpaper patterns

If you look carefully at wallpaper you will see the pattern repeated over and over again.

The design artist might choose a simple motif, like a flower and then move it about on a parallelogram tiling to get a pleasing pattern.

In practice, the artist is likely to place the flowers on a coordinate grid.

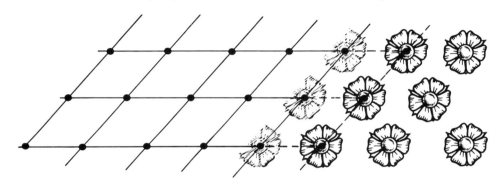

1 a Copy and continue this pattern on squared paper.
  b Write down the coordinates of flowers with y-coordinates of:
    (i) 0   (ii) 2   (iii) 4
  c Can you place a flower on the line $y = 3$?
  d Make up a rule for placing the flowers in position.
  e Will there be flowers at:
    (i) $(0, 18)$ (ii) $(2, 28)$ (iii) $(3, 20)$
    (iv) $(4, 38)$?

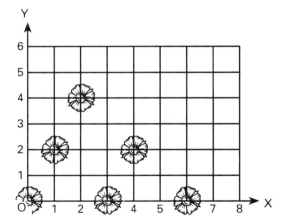

2 A leaf has to be placed at the intersection of the diagonals of each parallelogram of flowers.
  a Write down the coordinates of five leaves.
  b Make up a rule for placing the leaves in position.

3 In a different tiling, $(4, 0)$ and $(1, 3)$ are opposite corners of a parallelogram.
  a Make a diagram and find where the diagonals intersect.
  b Write down the coordinates of three pairs of points which could be the remaining corners of the parallelogram.

4 Bob and Sam are members of the region's road maintenance team. They are marking off a central line on the road for painting, so they use a chalked rope stretched across the road.
Explain how they do the job, and why the method works.

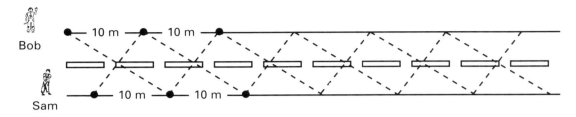

EXERCISE 5F

---

1 ACDG is a rectangle. Name two pairs of congruent trapezia in the diagram.

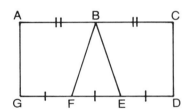

2

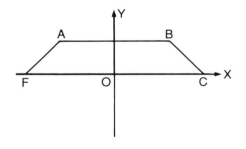

Trapezium ABCF is symmetrical about the y-axis and $\angle\,BCF = 45°$.
a Copy the diagram and complete it so that figure ABCDEF is symmetrical about both x and y-axes.
b A has coordinates $(-3, 2)$. Write down the coordinates of B, C, D, E and F.

3 The kitchen knife-holder is a wooden block with trapezium-shaped sides. Each edge is at 45° to the horizontal.
a What is the angle between PS and the vertical?
b Calculate the length of PQ.

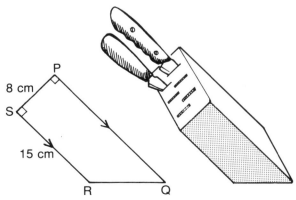

4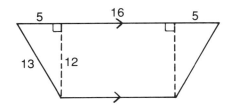

The lengths of this metal plate are in centimetres.

Calculate: **a** its perimeter   **b** its area.

5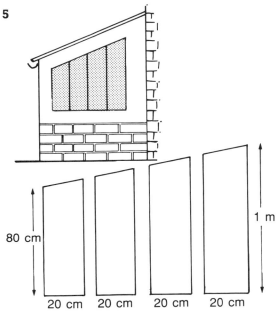

Mr Singh needs four pieces of glass for his lean-to porch.

a What shape is each piece?

b How can he cut the pieces from a single rectangular piece with no waste? Show this by means of a diagram.

c Calculate its area.

d Check the area, using a trapezium shape.

EXERCISE 6F

---

1 Plants grow up a garden trellis. Part of the trellis is shown. AB ∥ DC.

a What other fact would make ABCD a parallelogram?

b Without other information than AB ∥ DC, what kinds of quadrilateral could it be?

c ∠BAD = 75°. Copy the trellis, assuming it is made of parallelogram shapes, and fill in all the angles.

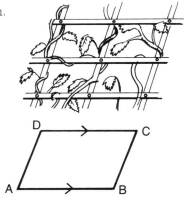

2 Susie is making a corner cabinet of
plywood, with one shelf.
   a List all the parts, with their dimensions.
   Ignore the thickness of the wood.
   b Calculate the total area of plywood that
   she needs.

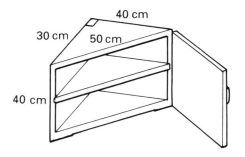

3 Which kind of quadrilateral goes in each box?

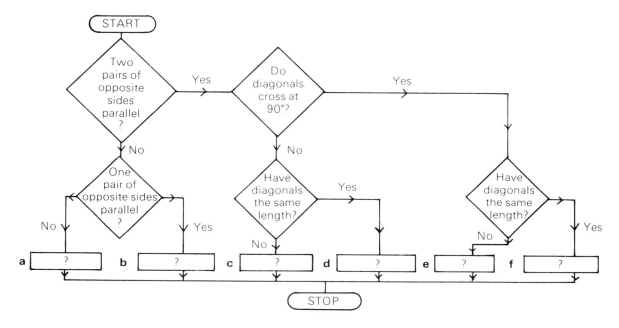

15 SOME SPECIAL NUMBERS

EXERCISE 1F

1 Which is the greater number in each pair?
  a 11^2 or 5^3 **b** 10^2 or 2^7 **c** 8^2 or 2^6 **d** 10^1 or 1^{10} **e** 4^4 or 6^3

2 Find the missing input and output numbers.

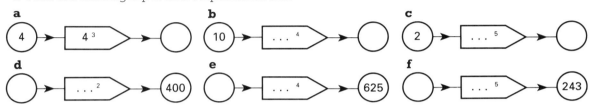

3 Find the value of the index n in each of these.
  a $2^n = 16$ **b** $13^n = 13$ **c** $4^n = 16$ **d** $7^n = 343$ **e** $10^n = 100\,000$

4 a Copy and complete:
  (i) $2^3 \times 2^4 = 2 \times \ldots \times \ldots \times 2 \times \ldots \times \ldots \times \ldots = 2^{\cdots}$
  (ii) $3^2 \times 3^4 = 3 \times \ldots \times 3 \times \ldots \ldots = 3^{\cdots}$
  (iii) $5^3 \times 5^3 = 5 \times \ldots \ldots = 5^{\cdots}$
  (iv) $6^2 \times 6^4 = 6^{\cdots}$
  (v) $10^5 \times 10^3 = \ldots$
  b Explain the rule for writing $2^7 \times 2^3$ as a single power of 2.
  c Write $2^a \times 2^b$ as a single power of 2.

5 $2^5 \div 2^3 = \dfrac{\cancel{2} \times \cancel{2} \times \cancel{2} \times 2 \times 2}{\cancel{2} \times \cancel{2} \times \cancel{2}} = 2 \times 2 = 2^2$ **a** Copy and complete:

  (i) $3^6 \div 3^3 = \dfrac{3 \times \ldots \ldots}{3 \times \ldots \ldots} = 3^{\cdots}$

  (ii) $4^5 \div 4^4 = \dfrac{4 \times \ldots \ldots}{4 \times \ldots \ldots} = 4^{\cdots}$

  (iii) $6^5 \div 6^2 = \ldots \ldots = 6^{\cdots}$
  (iv) $10^8 \div 10^4 = 10^{\cdots}$
  (v) $2^{10} \div 2^1 = \ldots$

  b Explain the rule for writing $3^8 \div 3^2$ as a single power of 3.
  c Write $2^a \div 2^b$ as a single power of 2.

6 a Use the rule in question **5** to write $2^5 \div 2^5$ as a single power of 2.
  b Explain why $2^0 = 1$.
  c Write down the value of: (i) 3^0 (ii) 10^0 (iii) x^0.

EXERCISE 2F

1 Find the missing 'in' and 'out' numbers:

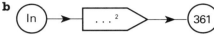

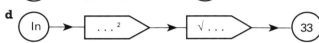
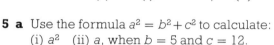

2 Calculate, correct to 3 significant figures:
  a 4.36^2 **b** 23.8^2 **c** $\sqrt{70}$ **d** $\sqrt{700}$

3 What is the greatest square number which is less than: **a** 1000   **b** 100 000?

4 The minimum speed v m/s for the roller coaster to loop-the-loop is given by the formula $v = \sqrt{10r}$ where r is the radius of the loop.
  Calculate, correct to 1 decimal place:
  a the speed (v) for: (i) $r = 8.1$ m   (ii) $r = 15$ m
  b the radius (r) for: (i) $v = 14$ m/s   (ii) $v = 19.5$ m/s

5 a Use the formula $a^2 = b^2 + c^2$ to calculate:
     (i) a^2 (ii) a, when $b = 5$ and $c = 12$.
  b Repeat **a**, giving your answer correct to 1 decimal place, when $b = 14$ and $c = 25$.

6 Use a trial and improvement method to solve:
  a $x^3 = 700$ **b** $x^2 - 3x = 75$,
  each correct to 3 decimal places.

7 A cube has a surface area of 300 cm².
  Use a trial and improvement method to calculate the length of one edge, correct to 3 significant figures.

EXERCISE 3F

1 The hour hand on the clock will point to 12 again in 12 hours' time.
  Will it point to 12 again in:
  a 24 hours   **b** 48 hours   **c** 80 hours
  d 100 hours   **e** 108 hours   **f** 144 hours?

2 A hand of the clock will point to 12 again after turning through 360°.
Which of these turns will point it to 12 again?

   a 540°   **b** 720°   **c** 900°   **d** 1000°   **e** 1080°

3 List the multiples of the numbers on the envelopes until you have two common multiples.
Say which is the least common multiple (lcm).

a    **b**    **c**

4 Find the lcm of each set of numbers:

a    **b**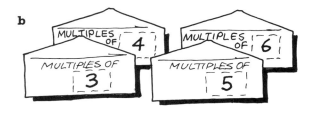

5 A company produces video tapes of various lengths.
This tape is meant for 20 minute or 30 minute programmes.
The shortest length of tape possible, without waste, is 60 minutes.
(3 × 20 minutes or 2 × 30 minutes.)
Find the shortest playing times for these lengths of programmes.

a   **b**   **c**   **d**

6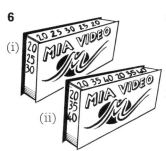

a The MIA video company wants to make a new tape designed to record 20 minute, 25 minute and 30 minute programmes without waste. Their research scientists tell them that $4\frac{3}{4}$ hours is the maximum possible playing time for any tape.
Is it possible for the company to make this new tape?

b Is tape (ii) possible, with a $4\frac{3}{4}$ hour maximum playing time?

EXERCISE 4F

List all the factors in each envelope.

1 THE FACTORS OF **28**

2 THE FACTORS OF **36**

3 THE FACTORS OF **40**

4 THE FACTORS OF **60**

5 THE FACTORS OF **64**

6 THE FACTORS OF **120**

Highest common factor (hcf)
The factors of 24 are 1, 2, 3, 4, 6, 8, 12, 24.
The factors of 32 are 1, 2, 4, 8, 16, 32.
The common factors of 24 and 32 are 1, 2, 4 and 8. Their *highest common factor* is 8.

List: **a** the factors   **b** the common factors
       c the highest common factor, of the numbers on each pair of envelopes:

7 THE FACTORS OF **12**   THE FACTORS OF **18**

8 THE FACTORS OF **28**   THE FACTORS OF **42**

9 THE FACTORS OF **24**   THE FACTORS OF **36**

Find the highest common factor of:
10 40, 60   **11** 40, 48   **12** 72, 84   **13** 54, 90
14 75, 125   **15** 64, 144   **16** 150, 180   **17** 60, 90, 135

18 Find the highest common factor of the pair of numbers in each fraction.
Use it to simplify the fraction.
a $\frac{28}{35}$ **b** $\frac{45}{60}$ **c** $\frac{84}{120}$ **d** $\frac{375}{1000}$ **e** $\frac{650}{1000}$ **f** $\frac{250}{1200}$

EXERCISE 5F

1 Which of these are prime numbers?
  a 147   **b** 153   **c** 209   **d** 223   **e** 401
  f 577   **g** 653   **h** 1001   **i** 1667   **j** 1999

2 Find the first term in each of these sequences which is not a prime number.
  a $2^2+7, 4^2+7, 6^2+7, \ldots$ **b** $3^2-2, 5^2-2, 7^2-2, \ldots$ **c** $2^3-1, 2^5-1, 2^7-1, \ldots$

3 Investigate the effectiveness of this prime number machine for input numbers from 1 to 20.

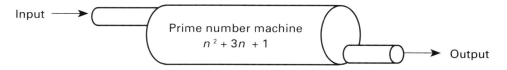

4 a Even numbers from 2 to 20 are fed into the machine. List the prime numbers that emerge.

Numbers in (values of n)

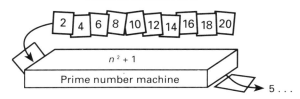

b The machine is reprogrammed to work out values of $2n^2 - 1$ and $2^n - 1$. When all the numbers from 2 to 10 are fed in, which programme produces more prime numbers?
Hint   When $n = 2$, $2n^2 - 1 = 2 \times 2^2 - 1 = 8 - 1 = 7$; $2^n - 1 = 2^2 - 1 = 3$.

5 Brainstormer
Find the greatest prime number which is less than 10 000. Explain your method for checking whether or not it is prime.

EXERCISE 6F

Write each number as a product of prime factors.
  1 24   **2** 30   **3** 40   **4** 66   **5** 70
  6 81   **7** 92   **8** 95   **9** 120   **10** 200

The least common multiple (lcm) of numbers can be found by means of prime factors.

$\left.\begin{array}{l} 12 = \mathbf{2} \times \mathbf{2} \times \mathbf{3} \\ 30 = \mathbf{2} \times 3 \times \mathbf{5} \end{array}\right\}$ so the lcm of 12 and 30 is $2 \times 2 \times 3 \times 5 = 60$.

Use prime factors to find the lcm of:
11 8, 10   **12** 15, 20   **13** 18, 20   **14** 24, 32   **15** 28, 35

Write each number as a product of prime factors in index form.
16 18   **17** 48   **18** 120   **19** 144   **20** 1024
21 225   **22** 324   **23** 4900   **24** 12 500   **25** 2744

16 FORMULAE AND SEQUENCES

EXERCISE 1F

1 A 50-cup teapot

a

HOW MANY CUPS ARE LEFT AFTER 6 HAVE BEEN POURED?

b

HOW MANY CUPS ARE LEFT AFTER 12 HAVE BEEN POURED?

   c Write down a formula for the number of cups (N) that are left after x cups have been poured.

   d Change your formula in **c** for a teapot holding: (i) 90 cups   (ii) C cups.

2

a I TRAVEL 10 KM PER LITRE OF PETROL. I'VE TRAVELLED 30 km. HOW MANY LITRES HAVE I USED?

b I TRAVEL 7 KM PER LITRE OF PETROL. I'VE TRAVELLED 77 km. HOW MANY LITRES HAVE I USED?

c I TRAVEL 5 KM PER LITRE OF PETROL. I'VE TRAVELLED 85 km. HOW MANY LITRES HAVE I USED?

   d (i) Write down a formula for the number of litres of petrol (N) used by a vehicle that travels d km at k km per litre.

      (ii) If the vehicle had S litres in its tank at the start of the journey find a formula for the number of litres (R) remaining in its tank.

3

a 12 WORDS PER LINE. 50 LINES PER PAGE. 40 PAGES PER NOTEBOOK. HOW MANY WORDS IN A BOOK?

b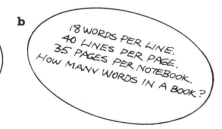

18 WORDS PER LINE. 40 LINES PER PAGE. 35 PAGES PER NOTEBOOK. HOW MANY WORDS IN A BOOK?

   c (i) Write down a formula for the number of words (N) in a notebook with W words to a line, L lines to a page and P pages in the book.

      (ii) A carton contains B notebooks. Find formulae for the number of pages (X) in a carton, lines (Y) in a carton and words (Z) in a carton.

4 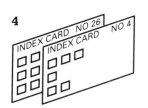 The cards have 1 cm² holes punched in them for filing purposes.

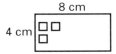
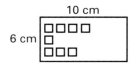

a What area is left?   **b** What area is left?

c Write down a formula for the area (A cm²) of a card L cm long and B cm broad after n holes have been punched in it.

d What would the formula be for holes with sides: (i) 2 cm long   (ii) x cm long?

5 Quick conversions. Make a formula for each, and use it for the calculations.
  a Feet (F) to metres (M): multiply by 3, then divide by 10. If $F = 5$, find M.
  b Kilometres (K) to miles (M): multiply by 5, then divide by 8. If $K = 32$, find M.
  c Degrees Fahrenheit (F) to Celsius (C): subtract 32, multiply by 5, then divide by 9. If $F = 212$, find C.

6 a x adults and y children buy tickets. Write down a formula for the total cost (£T).
  b If the total cost is £U, and only adults buy tickets, write down a formula for the number of adults (x).
  c If the total cost is £V, and x adults and y children buy tickets, write down a formula for the number of adults.

7 a The ferry sails at x km/h towards the coast which is y km away. Write down a formula for the distance (d km) to sail after: (i) h hours   (ii) m minutes.
  b What would your formulae be if the ferry sailed 2 km/h faster?

EXERCISE 2F

1 Make a formula for the perimeter (P) of each shape. The lengths are in millimetres.

a 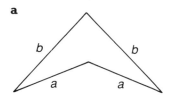   **b** 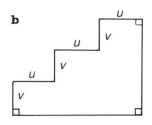   **c**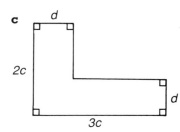

2 Make a formula for the perimeter of each pane of glass and for the whole window frame. Lengths are in centimetres.

a 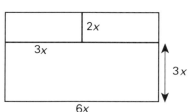   **b**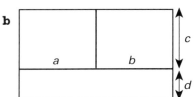

3 A rectangular conservatory floor is covered with square tiles of side s cm. There are r rows of tiles, each containing t tiles. Find a formula for the perimeter P of the floor.

4 Make a formula for the area (A) of each shape. The lengths are in centimetres.

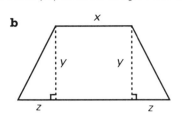 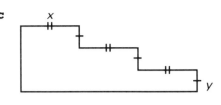

5 Make a formula for the area of each pane of glass and for the whole window in parts **a** and **b** of question **2**.

6 A cuboid is $3y$ cm long, $2y$ cm broad and y cm high. Find formulae for:
   a the total length of its edges   **b** its surface area   **c** its volume.

7 A water storage tank in the shape of a cuboid is x mm long, y mm broad and z mm high. The water in it is d mm deep. Find two formulae for the volume (V) of air in the tank.

EXERCISE 3F

1 To the right is an excerpt from an old catalogue.

   Give the rule and the next 3 entries in each column.

	TIPCO SOCKETS		American A/F sizes	
Stock No.	Nut size A/F (inches)	UNF Size (inches)	Socket end	Price (pence)
A14	$\frac{7}{16}$	$\frac{1}{4}$	0.64	69
A16	$\frac{1}{2}$	$\frac{5}{16}$	0.73	72
A18	$\frac{9}{16}$	$\frac{3}{8}$	0.81	75
A20	$\frac{5}{8}$	$\frac{7}{16}$	0.88	78
↓	↓	↓	↓	↓
a	**b**	**c**	**d**	**e**

2 In these sequences, each number is the sum of the two previous numbers. Complete:
   a 1, 1, 2, 3, 5, 8, . . . , . . . , . . . , 55, . . .
   b 4, 1, 5, 6, 11, . . . , . . . , . . . , . . . , 118, . . .
   c . . . , . . . , 7, 12, 19, 31, . . . , . . . , 131, . . . , . . .
   d . . . , . . . , . . . , 7, 11, 18, . . . , . . . , 76, . . . , . . .
   e 1, . . . , . . . , 9, . . . , 23, 37, . . . , 97, . . . , . . .

3 Here is an example of an old 'aptitude test'. You have to find the missing number in each sequence. The answers are upside down below. Try the test.

  a Check your answers. How many correct answers have you?

  b Now explain all the rules you used to answer the test.

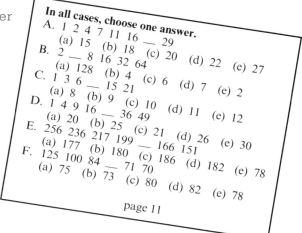

In all cases, choose one answer.
A. 1 2 4 7 11 16 — 29
  (a) 15 (b) 18 (c) 20 (d) 22 (e) 27
B. 2 — 8 16 32 64
  (a) 128 (b) 4 (c) 6 (d) 7 (e) 2
C. 1 3 6 — 15 21
  (a) 8 (b) 9 (c) 10 (d) 11 (e) 12
D. 1 4 9 16 — 36 49
  (a) 20 (b) 25 (c) 21 (d) 26 (e) 30
E. 256 236 217 199 — 166 151
  (a) 177 (b) 180 (c) 186 (d) 182 (e) 78
F. 125 100 84 — 71 70
  (a) 75 (b) 73 (c) 80 (d) 82 (e) 78

page 11

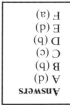

Answers
A (d)
B (b)
C (c)
D (b)
E (d)
F (a)

4 Complete, using the given rules:

  a . . ., . . ., . . ., 2, . . ., . . ., . . ., ... Double the previous number.

  b . . ., . . ., . . ., . . ., −1, 3, 2, . . ., . . ., ... Add the two previous numbers.

  c . . ., . . ., . . ., 5, . . ., . . ., ... Square the previous number, then add 1.

  d 89, 145, . . ., . . ., . ., . . ., . . ., . . ., . . ., . . ., . . ., ... Square each digit of the previous number, and find the total. (Any comments on further numbers?)

  e 7, 22, 11, . . ., ... If the previous number is odd then multiply it by three and add 1, otherwise halve it. Find the 'fate' of this sequence as it goes on, ...

Challenge
Some much harder rules to try to discover:

  A 1, 2, 4, 8, 16, 23, 28, 38, 49, 62, 70, 77, . . .

  B 345, 379, 416, 457, 502, . . .

  C 4, 6, 10, 14, 22, 26, 34, 38, 46, 58, 62, 74, . . .

  D 125, 129, 133, 142, 158, 183, 247, 263, 299, . . .

EXERCISE 4F

---

1 Find which term the given number is in each sequence.

a

689

b

567

c
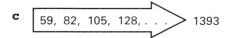
1393

d

8348

2 Here is a spreadsheet:

	A	B
1	5	
2	6	
3	7	
4	8	

The formula $2 \times A1 + 1$ placed in cell B1 gives $2 \times 5 + 1 = 11$. Can you see why?

The formula $3 \times A4 - 2$ placed in cell B4 gives $3 \times 8 - 2 = 22$. Explain why.

The spreadsheet now looks like this:

Note that the formulae are hidden—only the result shows.

	A	B
1	5	11
2	6	
3	7	
4	8	22

Show what these spreadsheets look like after these formulae are entered in the cells:

a

	C	D
1	1	$\leftarrow 2 \times C1 + 3$
2	2	$\leftarrow 2 \times C2 + 3$
3	3	$\leftarrow 2 \times C3 + 3$
4	4	$\leftarrow 2 \times C4 + 3$

b

	P	Q
1	7	$\leftarrow 5 \times P1 - 3$
2	8	$\leftarrow 5 \times P2 - 3$
3	9	$\leftarrow 5 \times P3 - 3$
4	10	$\leftarrow 5 \times P4 - 3$

3

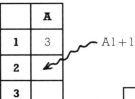

	A
1	3
2	
3	
4	
5	

$A1 + 1$

If this formula is copied down the column, then $A2 + 1$, $A3 + 1$ and $A4 + 1$ enter the cells A3, A4 and A5.
Explain why 4, 5, 6 and 7 appear in the cells of column A.
What numbers appear in the cells of these spreadsheets?

a

	A	B
1	3	
2		
3		
4		
5		

b

	A	B
1	5	
2		
3		
4		
5		

In A2 goes $A1 + 1$ and is copied down column A.
In B1 goes $3 \times A1 - 4$ and is copied down column B.

In A2 goes $A1 - 1$ and is copied down column A.
In B1 goes $7 \times A1 + 3$ and is copied down column B.

EXERCISE 5F

1   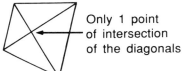 $x°$ and $y°$ form a pair of supplementary angles ($x° + y° = 180°$.)

a How many pairs of supplementary angles are formed when:
(i) 2 lines cross   (ii) 3 lines cross?

b Copy and complete this table:

No. of crossing lines	2	3	4	5	6
No. of pairs of supplementary angles			24	40	60

c Predict the number of pairs of supplementary angles for 8 crossing lines.

2

Only 1 point of intersection of the diagonals

a Find the *maximum* number of points of intersection of the diagonals of a pentagon.

b Copy and complete this table:

No. of sides of polygon	3	4	5	6	7	8	9
Maximum number of points of intersection of diagonals	0	1		15	35	70	126

c Can you predict the maximum number of points of intersection of the diagonals of a duodecagon (12-sided polygon)?

17 PROBABILITY

EXERCISE 1F

1 The diagram shows the position of Ian's counter.
A dice is rolled to see if he wins or loses.
   a Calculate: (i) P(W)   (ii) P(L).
   b Draw a tree diagram.

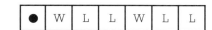

2 A bag contains red and white counters.
The tree diagram shows the probabilities
when one is taken out at random. There
are 4 red counters in the bag. Calculate:
   a the number of white counters
   b the total number of counters in the bag.

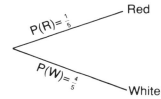

3 A set of traffic lights shows red for 20 seconds, amber for 10 seconds and green for 30 seconds.
Draw a tree diagram to show the probability of meeting each colour when Mrs Ford arrives at the lights.

4 In a marathon, the organisers expect three times more entrants to finish than not to finish.
   a Draw a tree diagram to show the probabilities involved.
   b If 600 finish how many failed to finish?

5 In a survey of 100 students, 35 have brown eyes, 28 have green eyes, 12 have blue eyes and the rest have grey eyes. Draw a tree diagram to show the probabilities of having the various colours of eyes.

6 The pie chart shows the crisp sales in the
school shop. Draw a tree diagram to show
the probabilities when one packet is
bought.

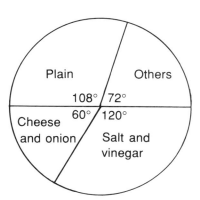

EXERCISE 2F

1 Copy the probability scale.

```
┌──┬──┬──┬──┬──┬──┬──┬──┬──┬──┐
0                 0.5                    1
```

A number from 1 to 20 is chosen at random. On the scale, mark the probability that the number is:

a even   **b** a multiple of 4   **c** a prime number
d a square number   **e** 21   **f** 6 or greater.

2 A survey shows that the probability that a household, chosen at random, has a freezer is 0.77.
   a What is the probability that a household will not have a freezer?
   b Draw a tree diagram of the probabilities.

3 Central High PTA sell 800 raffle tickets. There is one cash prize and there are nine other prizes.
   a Calculate the probability that Jim, with one ticket, will win:
      (i) a cash prize   (ii) any prize.
   b What is the probability that he will not win a prize?

4 In Lisa's class the probability of a pupil arriving at school early is 75% and late 5%.
   a Calculate the probability that a pupil arrives just on time.
   b Illustrate the probabilities in a tree diagram.

5 Use arrows on a probability scale to show these probabilities on a spin of the wheel.
   a P(winning £100)
   b P(winning £50)
   c P(losing)
   d P(winning some amount of money)
   e P(winning £150)

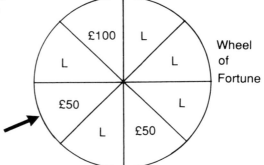

Wheel of Fortune

EXERCISE 3F

Describe in detail the method you would use to estimate these probabilities. Explain how and where you might obtain data.

1 A birth being triplets, quadruplets, and so on . . .

2 A ball landing on a black even number of a roulette wheel.

3 A mustard and cress seed from a packet failing to germinate.

4 A second-class letter arriving before a first-class letter when sent to the same address.

5 A person at a fair throwing six 6's to win a car.

6 A car, chosen at random in your area, being over 5 years old.

7 A space-probe being hit by an asteroid.

8 The candidate of a particular party winning in your area at the next General Election.

EXERCISE 4F

1 Out of 1000 pupils, about how many would you expect to be born on:
   a a Tuesday   **b** in April   **c** on Christmas Day   **d** on February the 29th?

2 The figures show the estimates of colour-blindness.
Estimate the number of:

Men	2% to 6%
Women	1%

   a men
   b women
   who are likely to be colour-blind out of 1000 people (500 male, 500 female).

3 A factory which makes golf balls regularly tests 50 000 of its product and finds that, generally, 300 fail its quality control test.
If a sports shop buys 2000 balls from the factory, approximately how many might be of poor quality?

4 New car registration numbers run from 1 to 999.
Out of one million, approximately how many would you expect to have:
   a only 1 digit   **b** only 2 digits   **c** three digits, all the same?

5 100 people qualify for a free spin of this wheel of fortune.
Calculate the amount of money the organisers should expect to pay out in prizes.

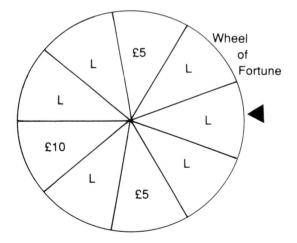

ANSWERS

1 NUMBERS IN ACTION

PAGE 1   EXERCISE 1F

1a (i) 78 340 000 km   (ii) 628 730 000 km
b 377 540 000 km   **c** 455 880 000 km
2a 2   **b** 11   **c** 21   **3b** (i) 200 m/s   (ii) 28 m/s
(iii) 1 m/s   **c** ÷1000, ×60, ×60   **d** (i) 72 km/h
(ii) 270 km/h   (iii) 29 km/h
4a (i) 115   (ii) 181   **b** (i) 5   (ii) 3

PAGE 2   EXERCISE 2F

1a (i) 9000 m, 5000 m   (ii) 8800 m, 4800 m
(iii) 8850 m, 4810 m   **b** (i) 4041 m   (ii) 4040 m
(iii) 4000 m   **2a** (i) 12 760 km   (ii) 12 800 km
(iii) 13 000 km   **b** (i) 6790 km   (ii) 6800 km
(iii) 7000 km   **c** (i) 142 980 km   (ii) 143 000 km
(iii) 143 000 km
3a Nearest 10 000   **b** nearest 100 000
4a Impossible to be so accurate   **b** for example:
916 000, 1 664 000, 3 880 000   **5a** 1382.5 million
b 1382 million   **c** 1380 million   **d** 1400 million

PAGE 2   EXERCISE 3F

1a 12.42   **b** 29.81   **c** 139.12   **d** 16.15
e 31.25 (marks)   **2a** 0.002 m³   **b** 0.014 m³
3a 6.45 and 6.55 cm   **b** 0.65 and 0.75 cm
c 13.05 and 13.15 cm   **d** 45.95 and 46.05 cm
4a 98 kg, 96 kg   **b** 12 kg, 10 kg
5 37.1 cm², 38.4 cm²   **6b** 11.42 cm   **7** 8.38 cm

PAGE 3   EXERCISE 4F

1a 2   **b** 3   **c** 3   **d** 1   **e** 3   **f** 1   **g** 6
2a 79 500   **b** 0.002   **c** 1.0   **d** 5.010   **e** 28.07
3a 5.3 cm   **b** 2   **4a** 1390 m²   **b** 8700 m³
5a 4.255, 0.7295; 4.265, 0.7305   **b** 3.10, 3.12 m²
6a 3   **b** 1670

PAGE 4   EXERCISE 5F

1a $(3 \times 5)^2$ **b** $(6 + 3 + 1)^2$ **c** $8 \times 5 + 3$ **d** $(10 - 1)^2$
e $(7 + 3) \times 8 - 5$ **f** $(12 + 4 \times 2)^3$ **2a** 75   **b** 10   **c** 64
d 9   **e** 30   **f** 44   **3a** 32   **b** 18   **c** 81   **d** 16   **e** 1
f 4   **g** 13   **h** 1125   **i** 36   **j** 216   **k** 1   **l** 56
4a $(8 - 2) \times 4 = 24$ **b** $(18 \div 6) \div 3 = 1$
c $(5 \times 2 + 3) \times 4 = 52$ **5a** (i) $48\,000 \div (757 - 397) =$
(ii) $757 - 397 = x \rightarrow M, 48\,000 \div MR =$
b (i) $64\,000 \div (357 + 456 + 787) =$
(ii) $357 + 456 + 787 = x \rightarrow M, 64\,000 \div MR =$
c (i) $85\,914 \div ((67 + 19) \times 27) =$
(ii) $67 + 19 = \times 27 = x \rightarrow M, 85\,914 \div MR =$
d (i) $3000 \div (4.5^2 + 6.5^2)$
(ii) $4.5^2 + 6.5^2 = x \rightarrow M, 3000 \div MR$

PAGE 5   EXERCISE 6F

1a 24   **b** 33   **c** 9   **d** 19   **e** 11
2a 120   **b** 140   **c** 96   **d** 216   **e** 720
3a 143   **b** 141   **c** 267   **d** 65   **e** 74
4a 160   **b** 630   **c** 1800   **d** 3200   **e** 490 000
5a 2   **b** 20   **c** 20   **d** 200   **e** 2000
6a 560   **b** 1014   **c** 234   **d** 114   **e** 616
7a 340   **b** 660   **c** 3700   **d** 7600   **e** 1560
8a 70   **b** 42   **c** 250   **d** 320
9a 2616   **b** 1512   **c** 3741   **d** 24 765   **e** 515 372
10a 34   **b** 54   **c** 32   **d** 68   **e** 38

2 ALL ABOUT ANGLES

PAGE 6   EXERCISE 1F

1 5°   **2a** 70° or 110°   **b** 20°
3a 30°   **b** 60°   **c** $67\frac{1}{2}°$ **d** 72°   **e** 54°   **4** $22\frac{1}{2}°$
5 ∠ABD and ∠CBF, ∠DBE and ∠EBF   ($x = 18°$)
6a 75°   **b** $(90 - y)°$ **c** $(90 - 2a)°$ **d** $(45 + y)°$
e $(10 + x)°$ **7a** $27\frac{1}{2}°$ **b** $11\frac{1}{2}$ more minutes

PAGE 6   EXERCISE 2F

1a 77° or 103°   **b** 13°   **2a** and **h**, **b** and **d**, **c** and **g**,
e and **f**   **3a** (i) ∠EBC   (ii) ∠EBG   (iii) ∠FBD
b (i) ∠DBC, ∠ABG   (ii) ∠ABG, ∠CBD   **c** 140°
4a 135°   **b** (i) 150°   (ii) 105°   (iii) 60°   (iv) 15°
5a 100°   **b** $(180 - x)°$ **c** $(180 - 2x)°$ **d** $(90 + 2y)°$
e $(80 - a)°$ **6** $5\frac{1}{2}$ minutes past 7 o'clock

PAGE 8   EXERCISE 3F

1a $a + b = 180, a + d = 180, b + c = 180, c + d = 180,$
$a = c, b = d, a + b + c + d = 360$ **b** c decreased by 30,
b and d increased by 30,   **c** a is doubled,
b and d reduced by c **2** 20°
3 6   ∠BOC and ∠FOE, ∠COD and ∠AOF,
∠DOE and ∠BOA, ∠BOD and ∠AOE,
∠COE and ∠BOF, ∠DOF and ∠AOC   **4a** (i) 4
(ii) 4   (iii) 4   **b** (i) 8   (ii) 8   (iii) 8

PAGE 8   EXERCISE 4F

1

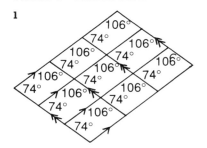

2 ∠NSQ = ∠RPM (corresponding angles, SK ∥ PR)
∠SQN = ∠PMR (corresponding angles, NQ ∥ KM)
∠SNQ = ∠SKM = ∠PRM (corresponding angles)
3 ∠ABC = 140°

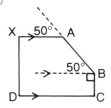

4 Draw a line from B to E, and continue it, or draw FE
further to meet AB, or draw DE further to meet BC.
Then use pairs of equal corresponding angles.
5a $a = 60, b = c = 60$ **b** $d = 130, e = 50, f = 65$

PAGE 9   EXERCISE 5F

1a 60° **b** 61° **c** 59° **2**

3 ∠TRP = 65°, ∠RSQ = 85°, ∠SQU = 85°,
∠SQR = 30° **4** ∠ABC = 88°, ∠DBC = 42°,
∠BDC = 50°
5a, c   **b** 8 **d** They are all equal to 180°.

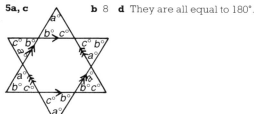

6 $x = 130, y = 230$
7 82° **8a** $a = 87, b = 87, c = d = 46\frac{1}{2}, e = 87;$
b $f = g = 53, h = 37, j = k = 53$

PAGE 11   EXERCISE 6F

1a Comp. 10, 11; supp. 2, 5; vert. opp. 8, 9;
corr. 1, 3 and 3, 4 and 2, 8 and 7, 8;
alt. 1, 2 and 5, 6 and 2, 4 and 7, 9 **b** Comp. 8, 9;
supp. 3, 4 and 5, 6 and 5, 11; vert. opp. 1, 10 and 6, 11;
corr. 9, 10 and 2, 3; alt. 1, 9 and 5, 7
2

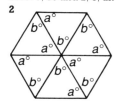

3a $a = 70, b = 65, c = 115, d = 45, e = 44, f = 91$,
b $g = 85, h = 95, i = 35, j = 60$

4a (i) ∠s BCF, BCR; RCD, FCD; DQP, CQP;
CQS, DQS (ii) ∠s DQP, CQS; BCF, DCR **b** (i) 142°
(ii) 52° (iii) 52°
5a ∠s ABE, BEF; ∠s BEF, EFI; ∠s HIF, IFJ
b ∠s CBE, BED
c

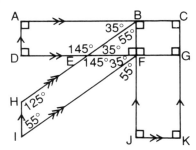

---

3 LETTERS AND NUMBERS

PAGE 12   EXERCISE 1F

1a $2y$ **b** y^2 **c** $3m$ **d** m^3 **e** $5a$ **f** $4a^2$ **g** $5b$
h $6b^2$ **i** c **j** $2d$ **k** $3n-5$ **l** $10k$ **m** $6t^2$ **n** $24a^3$
o $15cd$ **2a** $6 \times 6 \times 6$ **b** $10 \times 10 \times 10 \times 10$
c $y \times y \times y \times y \times y$ **d** $3 \times s \times s$ **e** $5 \times n \times n \times n$
f $2 \times a \times a \times b \times b$ **3** $b+2b = 3b, b \times 2b = 2b^2$;
$b+3, b \times 3, = 3b; b+5b = 6b, b \times 5b = 5b^2$;
$2b+3, 2b \times 3 = 6b; 2b+5b = 7b, 2b \times 5b = 10b^2$;
$3+5b, 3 \times 5b = 15b$ **4a** $2a$ **b** $2c$ **c** $2a+3$ **d** $2y$
5a $6t^2$ **b** a **c** $4v$ **d** $\frac{1}{4}x^2$
6a $2a, 2a^2, 2a^3, 2a^4, 2a^5$ **b** (i) $2a^3$ (ii) $2a$ or $2a^5$

Page 13   Investigation

1a 0 and 2 **b** t greater than 2 **c** t between 0 and 2
2a 2 and 4 **b** x between 2 and 4
c x between 0 and 2 and greater than 4.

PAGE 13   EXERCISE 2F

1a 9 **b** 5 **c** 18 **d** 15 **e** 8 **f** 35 **g** 27 **h** 10
i 45 **j** 18 **k** 14 **l** 30 **m** 21 **n** 45 **o** 55 **p** 51
2a 17 **b** 13 **c** 6 **d** 36 **e** 8 **f** 13 **g** 15 **h** 6
i 6 **j** 9 **k** 4 **l** 36 **m** 4 **n** 32 **o** 12 **p** 16
q 75 **r** 10 **s** 55 **t** 12 **u** 48 **v** 18 **w** 150 **x** 25
3a 8 **b** 16 **c** 16 **d** 8 **e** 6 **f** 13 **g** 6 **h** 13 **i** 6
j 16 **k** 6 **l** 16

Challenge

a, **d**; **b**, **c**; **e**, **g**; **f**, **h**; **i**, **k**; **j**, **l**

4a 2 **b** 3 **c** 2 **d** 2 **e** 9 **f** 9 **g** 2 **h** 2

PAGE 13   EXERCISE 3F

1a 15 km   **b** $7 + x$ km   **c** $15 + x$ km
2a $3x$ km   **b** $20 - 3x$ km   **c** $20 - x$ km
3a $5x$ km   **b** $120 - 6x$ km   **c** $120 - 3x$ km
4a $6, 2x + 10$ **b** $x + 3, 3x - 5$ **c** $2x + 8, x$
5 $T = 4t - 1$
6 $L = 200 - 15d$ **7a** $P = 8a, 8a, 18a, 20a$
b $P = 2p + 2s, 2p + 2r, 2q + 2r + 2s, 2p + 2q + 2r + 2s$
c $P = 6x + 200, 2x + 100, 300 - 2x, 6x + 300$
8 $P = 70s$ **9** Vegetables $P = 6y$; garage $P = 6y - 6$;
lawn $P = 6y + 4$; patio $P = 4y + 2$; hut $P = 2y$;
fruit $P = 4y - 4$
10a $A = 3a^2$ **b** $A = 3xy$ **c** $A = 12y^2$
11a $L = 12x$ **b** $A = 6y^2$ **c** $V = x^3$
12a $V = 4c^3$ **b** $\frac{2}{3}c$ cm

PAGE 15   EXERCISE 4F

1 $4(x + 3) = 4x + 12$ **2** $5(y + 2) = 5y + 10$
3 $6(x + y) = 6x + 6y$ **4** $7(a + b) = 7a + 7b$
5 $2(2x + 3) = 4x + 6$ **6** $10(3y + 4) = 30y + 40$
7 $7(4t + u) = 28t + 7u$ **8** $3(4y + 2x) = 12y + 6x$
9 $13(5c + 3d) = 65c + 39d$ **10** $x(y + 3) = xy + 3x$
11 $a(a + 4) = a^2 + 4a$ **12** $x(x + 1) = x^2 + x$

PAGE 16   EXERCISE 5F

1a $4 + x - x^2$ **b** $2m^2$ **c** $5x + 10$ **d** $y^3 + 3y$
e $a^3 - 5a$ **f** $2b^3 + b^2$ **g** $5c - c^3$ **h** $2x^3$
i $2ab - 3a + 3b$ **j** $7x - 5y + xy$ **k** $2y^3 - y^2 + y$
2a $x^2 + 3x + 2$ **b** $x^2 + 7x + 10$ **c** $y^2 + 4y + 4$
d $6x^2 + 9x + 3$ **e** $x^2 + 2xy + y^2$ **f** $15x^2 + 23x + 4$
3a $x^2 + xy + 2x + y + 1$ **b** $x^3 + 2x^2 + 2x + 1$

Page 16   Investigation

$$x + 1$$
$$x^2 + 2x + 1$$
$$x^3 + 3x^2 + 3x + 1$$ $3x^2$
$$x^4 + 4x^3 + 6x^2 + 4x + 1$$ Coefficient
$$x^5 + 5x^4 + 10x^3 + 10x^2 + 5x + 1$$

Each coefficient is the sum of the two coefficients
immediately above it. The coefficients form part of
Pascal's triangle.

4   MAKING SENSE OF STATISTICS 1

PAGE 17   EXERCISE 1F

1a 240 km/h, 6 seconds   **b** Four—before each one
the speed drops as the brakes are applied   **c** 44 s
2a 1984, 1985, 1988, 1989   **b** 1985; 100   **c** less by 260

3a 70 000 litres   **b** 456 000 litres   **c** (i) $\frac{2}{9}$ (ii) $\frac{22}{35}$
d Sales of full cream fell throughout the year as sales
of low fat rose. The sales were equal late in July.
Increasingly, low fat milk was considered best for
good health, so more people bought it.

PAGE 18   EXERCISE 2F

1a Non-uniform vertical scale, and no title.
b Optical illusion exaggerates apparent growth.
c Visually volume is suggesting growth of 8 times
while text says 2 times.   **d** Vertical scale not in
order.   **2** Rate slows, not increases.

PAGE 19   EXERCISE 3F

1a Northend   **b** Northend
2a 2.93 min   **b** 3.06 min, 0.13 min longer
3 (146 letters, 39 words . . . 346 letters, 79 words)
a 4.875, 9.875   **b** 3.7, 4.4

PAGE 20   EXERCISE 4F

1a 65 kg   **b** (i) 65 kg   (ii) 65.7 kg   (iii) 20 kg
2a Thursday, Wednesday   **b** (i) 6.5   (ii) Tue 6,
Wed 8.5, Thu 8, Fri 6.5, Sat 7, Sun 7   **c** (i) 5   (ii) 4
3a 3   **b** 2.625.

5   FRACTIONS, DECIMALS AND PERCENTAGES

PAGE 22   EXERCISE 1F

1 0.019, two hundredths, twenty two thousandths, 0.025
2a (i) 0.7   (ii) 70   **b** (i) 25   (ii) 2500   **c** (i) 0.026
(ii) 2.6   **3a** (i) 0.4   (ii) 0.004   **b** (i) 37   (ii) 0.37
c (i) 652   (ii) 6.52   **4a** 780   **b** 5 cm   **5** 580 g
6a £22.95   **b** £8.45   **c** £31.40   **7a** 87   **b** £26.78
c 1777

PAGE 23   EXERCISE 2F

1a A day   **b** cm   **c** gram   **d** second
2a $\frac{5}{6}$ **b** $\frac{3}{4}$ **c** $\frac{1}{3}$ **d** $\frac{6}{25}$ **e** $\frac{5}{6}$ **f** $\frac{2}{3}$
3a £2.10   **b** £1.20   **c** £20   **d** £30
4a $\frac{1}{4}$ **b** $\frac{11}{36}$ **c** $\frac{5}{24}$ **d** $\frac{8}{9}$ **e** $\frac{5}{12}$
5a 25p   **b** £12   **c** £24   **d** £2.56   **6a** 35%   **b** 65%
7a 18% of £250 by £3   **b** $\frac{11}{12}$ of 96p by 3p

PAGE 23   EXERCISE 3F

1a (i) £15   (ii) 3p   **b** (i) £10.10
(ii) Various possibilities: 76p for 5, 61p for 4,
91p for 6 . . . each makes just over £70

2a (i) £315 (ii) £65 **b** £380 **c** £330. Take cost of 1 record in each case. Was £$\frac{3}{2}$ ('Recent') and £$\frac{2}{3}$ ('Golden'), now £1 for each type. Loss £$\frac{1}{2}$ (total £150), gain £$\frac{1}{3}$ (total £100). Net loss £50
3a £5280, £4646.40, £4088.83, £3598.17
b Sunday, £2786.42
4a £110.40 **b** £155.33 **5** 4.3%
6a Smaller by 9 cm² **b** 1%

PAGE 24   EXERCISE 4F

1a (i) $\frac{8}{25}$ (ii) 0.32 **b** (i) $\frac{7}{50}$ (ii) 0.14 **c** (i) $\frac{13}{20}$
(ii) 0.65 **d** (i) $\frac{2}{25}$ (ii) 0.08 **e** (i) $\frac{1}{8}$ (ii) 0.125 **f** (i) $\frac{1}{50}$
(ii) 0.02 **2** 0.35, 36%, $\frac{74}{200}$, $\frac{19}{50}$ **3a** They are equal
b 15 cm ÷ 0.64 **4a** (i) 0.833 (ii) 83.3% **b** (i) 0.625
(ii) 62.5% **c** (i) 0.429 (ii) 42.9% **d** (i) 0.7
(ii) 70% **e** (i) 0.04 (ii) 4% **f** (i) 0.075 (ii) 7.5%
5a 15%, 0.15, $\frac{15}{100}$, $\frac{3}{20}$ **b** 5%, 0.05, $\frac{5}{100}$, $\frac{1}{20}$
c 64%, 0.64, $\frac{64}{100}$, $\frac{16}{25}$ **d** 12.5%, 0.125, $\frac{12.5}{100}$, $\frac{1}{8}$
6a 60%, $\frac{3}{5}$ **b** 19%, $\frac{19}{100}$ **c** 88.5%, $\frac{177}{200}$ **d** 8%, $\frac{2}{25}$
e 72%, $\frac{18}{25}$ **f** 0.3%, $\frac{3}{1000}$ **7a** $\frac{2}{9}$ **b** $\frac{1}{3}$ **c** $\frac{1}{11}$ **d** $\frac{2}{15}$

PAGE 25   EXERCISE 5F

1 Austria 25% (90°), Brazil 30% (108°), Cameroon 15% (54°), Denmark 10% (36°), Egypt 20% (72°) **2** Angles 180°, 65°, 50°, 43°, 22°
3 1.1% **4a** 87.5, 83.3% **b** A by 4.2%
5a (i) £90 000 (ii) £183 750 **b** 104%
6a £160 **b** £128 **c** £102.40 **7** 3
8a $\frac{35}{1000} = \frac{3.5}{100} = 3.5\%$, $\frac{0.16}{1000} = \frac{0.016}{100} = 0.016\%$,
$\frac{192}{1000} = \frac{19.2}{100} = 19.2\%$, $\frac{203}{1000} = \frac{20.3}{100} = 20.3\%$
b 10.754% or 107.54‰

---

6   DISTANCES AND DIRECTIONS

PAGE 27   EXERCISE 1F

1 195 m **2** 67 m **3** About 1000 m **4** 250 minutes

PAGE 28   EXERCISE 2F

1 43 km **2b** Both octagons **3a** 67$\frac{1}{2}$° **b** 45°
c 135° **d** 135°

PAGE 28   EXERCISE 3F

1 Aristarchus 320°, Alphonsus 125°, Bullialdus 180°, Copernicus 000°, Eratosthenes 030°, Gassendi 240°, Grimaldi 270°, Kepler 310°, Reinhold 350°.
2a (i) 240° (ii) 020° (iii) 180° + x° **b** 180° + x°, x° − 180° **3a** 085° **b** 060°

PAGE 29   EXERCISE 4F

1 210° for 6 km **2b** 1.7 km **c** 0.8 km **3a** 060°, 6 runs per minute gives 8 km. **b** (i) Loosestrife
(ii) Lupin (iii) Violet (iv) Primrose

---

7   POSITIVE AND NEGATIVE NUMBERS

PAGE 32   EXERCISE 1F

1a 7497 m **b** 267 m **c** 7200 m **d** 1940 m
e 19 840 m **f** 2260 m **2a** 53.8 **b** (i) 28.7° lower
(ii) 8.6° lower (iii) 15.6° higher (iv) 25.1° higher
c Moscow is 2.8° lower **d** July temp. is 40.4° higher
3 66.8 **4a** 69.5 **b** 94.6 **5c** $(1, -6), (-2, -4), (5, 2)$,
$(-4, -1), (4, -24), (a, -4-b)$ **6b** A kite **c** $(2, -6)$,
$(-7, 0), (-7, 3), (-4, 3)$. Their x and y coordinates are swapped and then their signs are changed.

PAGE 33   EXERCISE 2F

1a 1 **b** −1 **c** 4 **d** 0 **e** 1 **f** −6 **g** −1 **h** 1
i 10 **j** −8 **k** −9 **l** −9 **m** −x **n** −4y **o** 2a
p 5b **q** 0 **r** −3d **2a** −2 **b** −5 **c** 1 **d** 1
e 22 **f** 7 **g** −7 **h** −5 **i** −11 **j** 5 **k** 6 **l** 3
3 £2000, £3000, £1500, £3000, £4000, £2500; −15 000, −13 000, −10 000, −8500, −5500, −1500, 1000

PAGE 34   EXERCISE 3F

1a 3 **b** 3 **c** 5 **d** −4 **e** 0 **f** −2 **g** −4 **h** −6
i 0 **j** 0 **k** −7 **l** −2 **m** x **n** −y **o** −10a
p −2b **q** −7c **r** 3d
2a 5 **b** 1 **c** 7 **d** −2 **e** −1 **f** 5 **g** 0 **h** −2
3a

−5	0	−7
−6	−4	−2
−1	−8	−3

b

−8	−3	−10
−9	−7	−5
−4	−11	−6

c

−11	−6	−13
−12	−10	−8
−7	−14	−9

d centre number should be −2

4a −1 **b** −4 **c** −2 **d** 9 **e** −5 **f** −2
5a

−3	2	3	−4
4	1	−2	7
2	−3	−3	2
−1	6	4	1

b

−3	−2	1	0
22	2	−3	17
17	−3	12	32
−8	−7	16	15

c

5	5	−2	2
6	2	8	−4
−4	−6	−3	5
3	9	−7	1

6a (i) $-4-(-1) = -3$ or $-4-(-3) = -1$
(ii) $6-(-2) = 8$ or $6-8 = -2$
(iii) $-10-(-2) = -8$ or $-10-(-8) = -2$
(iv) no winners   (v) $6-(-1) = 7$ or $6-7 = -1$
(vi) $-5-4 = -9$ or $-5-(-9) = 4$
(vii) $-3-6 = -9$ or $-3-(-9) = 6$
(viii) $5-(-2) = 7$ or $5-7 = -2$
b (i) $3-x = -4$, $x = 7$, 7D or 7H
(ii) $x-(-5) = 7$, $x = 2$, 2D or 2H
(iii) $-6-x = -8$, $x = 2$, 2D or 2H
(iv) $3-x = -6$, $x = 9$, 9D or 9H
(v) $x-2 = -3$, $x = -1$; Ace of spades or
Ace of clubs

Page 36   Brainstormer

$-18°$C, $121°$C

PAGE 36   EXERCISE 4F

2a -15 **b** 15 **c** 1 **d** Ignore negative sign; take 3
and 4. Closest to zero is $4-3 = 1$: $3 \times$ larger $+$ smaller
gives maximum ($3 \times 4 + 3 = 15$). The negative gives
the minimum, -15.

ROUND IN CIRCLES

PAGE 37   EXERCISE 1F

1 4 cm **2a** (i) 4 mm (ii) 0.4 cm **b** $12\frac{1}{2}$
3a 0.9 mm **b** 2.8 (gauge 4) and 4.5 (gauge 2) **c** 6, 7
and 8, 10 **4a** (5, 2) **b** (−1, 1) **c** (1, 2), (−2, −1)
d (1, 2), radius 5; (2, −1), radius 5; (6, −13), radius 15;
(−3, 14), radius 15

PAGE 38   EXERCISE 2F

1a 2 cm, 6.28 cm **b** 80 **2a** 251 m **b** 23.9
c 16.8 m/s **3a** $\frac{1}{4}$ **b** 18.8 mm
4a 0.2 mm **b** 62.8 cm **c** 0.6 mm
5a 16.05 cm, 15.95 cm **b** 1

Page 38   Brainstormer

a 2.6 cm. Small washer's diameter is $\frac{2}{3}$ large washer's
diameter, since diameter of hole and width of large
washer are equal. **b** Arrive simultaneously (small
washer has $\frac{2}{3}$ circumference but $1\frac{1}{2}$ times number of
turns).

PAGE 39   EXERCISE 3F

1a 40.1 cm **b** 23.1 cm **c** 8.0 ft **2** 21.6 cm
3a 1.8 m **b** 57 cm **4a** 72 m **b** 40 **c** 2 m
d 31.8 cm **5** 180 cm

PAGE 40   EXERCISE 4F

1a 179 mm² **b** HS 220 and HS 190 **c** 1632 mm²
2a 201 mm² **b** 471 mm² **3a** (i) 252 km (ii) 7 **b** H

TYPES OF TRIANGLE

PAGE 41   EXERCISE 1F

1a $x = 15$; 30°, 60° **b** $x = 10$; 40°, 50°
c $x = 9$; 12°, 78° **d** $x = 20$; 20°, 70°; $y = 5$; 15°, 75°
2a Each sum is 180° **b** $x+90-x+y+90-y = 180$
3a $x = 30$; 120°, 10°, 50° **b** $x = 15$; 45°, 35°, 100°
c $x = 25$; 40°, 80°, 60° **4a** $x = 20$; $2x+50$ for $\angle$A,
$x+10$ for $\angle$B, $3x$ for $\angle$C **b** $x = 30$; $50-x$ for $\angle$D,
$4x$ for $\angle$E, $x+10$ for $\angle$F

PAGE 42   EXERCISE 2F

1a 4.75 m² **b** 3 m²
2a 29.58 cm² **b** 2.88 cm **3a** 24 km **b** D 225 m²,
A 220 m², C 80 m², B 75 m²

Page 42   Brainstormer

(1, 4), (7, 2), (10, 1), (13, 0). At (4, 0), $\frac{1}{2}$; (5, 0), 1; (6, 0), $1\frac{1}{2}$;
(0, 2), $1\frac{1}{2}$; (1, 2), 2; etc.

PAGE 43   EXERCISE 3F

1a $x = 11$; 77°, 77°, 26° **b** $x = 12$; 51°, 51°, 78°
2a They do not add up to 180°. **b** $x = 20$; 70°, 70°,
40°. Yes
3a $x = 20$, giving 75°, 30°, 75°. $(50-x)°$ is the odd one
b $x = 40$, giving 120°, 30°, 30°. $3x°$ is the odd one
4 $x = 10$; 20 cm, 20 cm, 34 cm
5 $x = 4$; 8 cm, 9 cm, 8 cm
$x = 4\frac{1}{2}$; 9 cm, $9\frac{1}{2}$ cm, $9\frac{1}{2}$ cm
$x = 5$; 10 cm, 10 cm, 11 cm

6a 1.8 m **b** 60 cm **c** 90 cm, 45 cm **d** (i) 1350 cm²
(ii) 1350 cm² **7** 781.5 mm²

PAGE 44   EXERCISE 4F

1a F_1 **b** F_2 **c** R_2 **d** R_1 **e** F_3

2

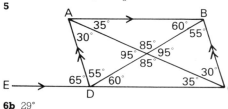

R_1	R_2	R_3	F_1	F_2	F_3
R_2	R_3	R_1	F_3	F_1	F_2
R_3	R_1	R_2	F_2	F_3	F_1
F_1	F_2	F_3	R_1	R_2	R_3
F_2	F_3	F_1	R_3	R_1	R_2
F_3	F_1	F_2	R_2	R_3	R_1

PAGE 45   EXERCISE 5F

1a $\angle A = 54°$, $\angle C = 36°$
b $\angle D = 60°$, $\angle E = 80°$, $\angle F = 40°$
c $\angle G = 125°$, $\angle H = 20°$, $\angle I = 35°$
2a Scalene **b** equilateral **c** right-angled
d isosceles **3** $\angle N = \angle M = 70°$, $\angle K = 40°$;
$\angle H = 45°$, $\angle I = \angle J = 67\frac{1}{2}°$ **4** $x = 8$
5

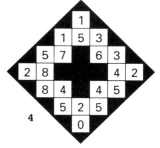

6b 29°

PAGE 46   EXERCISE 6F

1 North Farm **2** Hill Farm **3** Thorntree at 1400 m
and 1600 m, or Huntingtower at 1400 m and 1600 m.

PAGE 47   EXERCISE 7F

1a 1, 3, 6, 10, 15, 21, 28, 36, 45, 55 **b** Triangles of
dots **2a** 1, 3, 6, 10 **b** (i) 55 (ii) 210
c (i) 1 3 6 10 15 21   Totals, 1, 4, 10, 20, 35, 56

```
   1  3  6 10 15
      1  3  6 10
         1  3  6
            1  3
               1
```

(ii) 1540
3a 4, 12, 24, 60, 84.
Each is four times
a triangular number
b 840

4

---

10 METRIC MEASURE

PAGE 48   EXERCISE 1F

1a 15.4 cm **b** 9.2 cm **2** 63, 38, 28 mph
3a 6 km 880 m **b** 800 m **4a** 11.5 km **b** 11 500 m
5a 20.8 m **b** 1.05 m **c** 0.6 m **d** 0.54 m
6 1.015 km **7a** 4; 85 cm **b** 3; 2.4 m

Page 49   Investigation

Examples

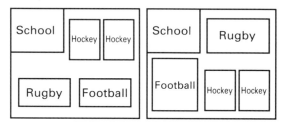

PAGE 49   EXERCISE 2F

1a 20.25 cm² **b** 1.28 m² or 12 800 cm² **2** 640 cm²
3 7050 m² **4** 625 **5** 100 **6** 80 **7** Yes, to 3
significant figures
8a (i) 3424 m (ii) 3.424 km **b** 380 m
c 45–50 hectares **9** 4 **10** 241

PAGE 50   EXERCISE 3F

1a 1368 cm³ **b** 1.62 m³ **2a** 17 cm **b** 6
3 4200 cm³ **4** 15 000 **5** $31\frac{1}{4}$ minutes
6a (i) 375 m³ (ii) 375 000 litres **b** 1 m 3 cm
7a 360 **b** 24

PAGE 51   EXERCISE 4F

1 7 **2a** 0.45 kg **b** 450 g **3a** 13.5 g **b** 2.7 kg
4a 500 **b** 36; 18 125 **c** 607; 22 000; 11 000 000 **5** 3 g
6 57p, 57p, 99p, 39p, 89p, £1.53; £4.94
7a (i) 192 cm³ (ii) 1536 cm³ **b** 12 kg
c 32 cm, 16 cm, 96 kg **d** 64 cm, 32 cm, 48 cm, 768 kg
e 48 kg **f** $1 \times 1 \times 192$, $1 \times 2 \times 96$, $1 \times 3 \times 64$, $1 \times 4 \times 48$,
$1 \times 6 \times 32$, $1 \times 8 \times 24$, $1 \times 12 \times 16$, $2 \times 2 \times 48$, $2 \times 3 \times 32$,
$2 \times 4 \times 24$, $2 \times 6 \times 16$, $2 \times 8 \times 12$, $3 \times 4 \times 16$, $3 \times 8 \times 8$,
$4 \times 4 \times 12$, $4 \times 6 \times 8$.

11 EQUATIONS AND INEQUATIONS

PAGE 53   EXERCISE 1F

1a $x = 4$; 20 cm, 3 cm, 17 cm
b $x = 6$; 17 cm, 7 cm, 10 cm
c $x = 3$; 5 cm, 3 cm, 5 cm, 7 cm
d $x = 3$; 1 cm, 13 cm, 1 cm, 11 cm
e $x = 2$; 14 cm, 5 cm, 7 cm, 7 cm, 9 cm, 2 cm
2a $2x$ m **b** 2 m 22 cm, 4 m 44 cm **c** 6 cm **d** 10 cm
e The sequence of sides is
3, 9, 18, 30, 45, 63, 84, 108, ... Solving $108x = 60$
gives a side length of 55 cm, with 60 cm over.
3a 8, 4, 4 cm **b** 18, 10, 8 cm **c** 4, 2, 2 cm
d 8, 10, 2 cm **e** $3\frac{1}{2}, \frac{1}{2}$, 4 cm **f** 12, 5, 7 cm or 4, 7, 3 cm
g $16\frac{1}{3}$, 7, $9\frac{1}{3}$ cm or 11, 15, 4 cm **h** No solutions **i** An
infinite number of possibilities for all $x > \frac{1}{3}$
4a 6, 2, 4, 4; 8 cm or 4, 1, 2, 1; 4 cm
b 7, 3, 8, 2; 10 cm or 3, 1, 6, 4; 7 cm
c 6, 1, 2, 3; 6 cm or $7\frac{1}{2}$, 4, 5, $1\frac{1}{2}$; 9 cm

Page 54   Brainstormers

1 $x = 1$ gives 9 cm length; $x = 4$ gives 24 cm lengths
2 1, 1, 2, 2, 4 cm or 2, 2, 4, 3, 1, 6 cm
$\frac{1}{2}, \frac{1}{2}, 1, 1\frac{1}{2}, 2\frac{1}{2}$, 3 cm or $\frac{1}{3}, \frac{2}{3}, 1\frac{1}{3}, 2\frac{2}{3}, 2\frac{2}{3}$ cm

PAGE 54   EXERCISE 2F

1a 1 **b** 3 **c** 10 **d** 2 **e** 51 **f** 11 **g** 5 **h** 6 **i** 3
j 5 **k** 5 **2a** (i) $4x + 22$ cm (ii) $8(2x + 3)$ cm^2
(iii) 56 cm^2 (iv) 26 cm **b** (i) $6x + 16$ cm
(ii) $10(3x - 2)$ cm^2 (iii) 130 cm^2 (iv) 58 cm
c (i) $2x + 26$ mm (ii) $18(x - 5)$ mm^2 (iii) 144 mm^2
(iv) 44 mm **d** (i) $4x + 16$ m (ii) $7(2x + 1)$ m^2
(iii) 133 mm^2 (iv) 44 m **3a** (i) $\frac{1}{2}(4x - 2 \times 5)$
(ii) $5(2x - 5)$ m^2 (iii) 16 m **b** 18 m **c** 40 m **d** 16 m

PAGE 56   EXERCISE 3F

1a $x \leqslant 30$ **b** $y > 30$ **2a** $x \geqslant 14$ **b** $y < 14$
3a $t > 2$ **b** $w \leqslant 2$ **4a** $x \geqslant 2$ **b** $y < 2$
5 $12 \leqslant y \leqslant 26$ **6** $2 \leqslant x < 12$; $160 < y \leqslant 200$

12 RATIO AND PROPORTION

PAGE 57   EXERCISE 1F

1a (i) 1:9, 1:4, 1:7, 1:8 (ii) butter, cherry, sponge,
shortbread **b** (i) 1:2, 1:3, 1:3, 1:4 (ii) cherry,
sponge and shortbread (equal), butter

2a (i) 1:21 (ii) 1:5 (iii) 1:3 **b** 1:2.33, 1:2, 1:1.8,
1:1.67, 1:1.57, 1:1.5, 1:1.44, 1:1.4
c the ratio gets closer to 1:1, for example
1000:1020 = 1:1.02 **3a** 6:3, 4:2, equal(2:1), so
balanced **b** 5:6, 5:4, not equal, not balanced
4a Both ratios 3:1, balanced **b** both ratios 2:5,
balanced **c** both ratios 7:3, balanced **d** 2:3, 7:10,
not balanced **5a** Add 2 to left **b** add 3 to right
c add 2 to right **d** add 1 to left
6a 20 cm from left **b** 15 cm from left
c 18 cm from left **d** 12 cm from left **7** To balance,
left weight:right weight = 28:36 = 7:9. So right
weight would be 54. 50 is too light, so left side goes
down

PAGE 58   EXERCISE 2F

1a 3 **b** 12 **c** 24 **d** 2 **e** 8 **f** 16
2a (i) 40 tonnes (ii) 76 tonnes (iii) 190 tonnes
b (i) 140 g (ii) 50 g (iii) 30 g **c** (i) 21:6 = 7:2,
so need oxygen content (ii) 21:7 = 3:1, so sample is
anthracite **3a** Ratio 3:6:4. Pay £1.20, £2.40, £1.60
b 30p, 60p, 40p **4a** (i) 6 cm, 8 cm (ii) 12 cm, 4 cm
b 6:1 **c** 2:3 **d** (i) 8 cm, 12 cm; 16 cm, 6 cm; 12:1;
3:4 (ii) 8 cm, 3 cm; 6 cm, 4 cm; 3:1; 4:3 **e** (i) xy:1
(ii) height y cm and width x cm

PAGE 59   EXERCISE 3F

1 5:1, 500:1, 600:1
2a 5 mm **b** 9 mm **c** 10 mm **d** 9 mm × 7.2 mm
3a 1.3 mm **b** 3 mm **c** 0.004 mm **d** 0.005 mm
4a 7.5:1 **b** 3.75:1, 375:1, 450:1
5 56.25:1, 14.06:1, 140 625:1, 202 500:1
6a A, B, E, F **b** (i) £2.40 (ii) £15

PAGE 60   EXERCISE 4F

1a 180 cm **b** 250 cm **c** 225 cm **2a** $33\frac{1}{3}$ mm
b £11 400 000 000 **3a** £18 **b** 220 km **c** (i) £12.50
(ii) £33.75 **5a** 60 kg **b** 0.4 cm

PAGE 61   EXERCISE 5F

1a £1.90 **b** $3.10 **c** 2.30 Cypriot pounds
2a 220 Maltese pounds **b** £110 **c** 65 NZ dollars
3 US dollars and NZ dollars **4** Scales could be £1 to
20 mm horizontally and 200 units of foreign currency
to 20 mm vertically. Then plot (1, 174) or (4, 696) for
Spain etc., and draw lines to the origin.

PAGE 62   EXERCISE 6F

1 261.6 Hz↔50 cm

$$440.0 \text{ Hz} \leftrightarrow 50 \times \frac{261.6}{400} \text{ cm} \doteqdot 29.7 \text{ cm}$$

2 Vibrating lengths (cm): D 44.5, E 39.6, F 37.5,
G 33.4, B 26.5, C′ 25.

PAGE 62   EXERCISE 7F

1a 1.5:1 **b** 2.25:1 **c** 3.375:1 **2** 6.12 m
3a 132 **b** 80 **4** 16.2 mins **5** 80 cm, 125 cm
6a 32 cm **b** 8.6 km **7** 8 **8** 172 852
9a 63.5 million **b** 3 968 750.

13 MAKING SENSE OF STATISTICS 2

PAGE 64   EXERCISE 1F

1a 5.0, 5, 6 **b** With a range of 5 hours and a mean of
5 hours, Jim is in the middle of the group.
2 *Forever* 3.9, *Hear Me* 4 **3a** Old 2800, New 4500
b The mean is 7300. Initially this did drop, but
quickly picked up

PAGE 65   EXERCISE 2F

1c 30–39 **d** $\frac{3}{10}$ **2a** 90 h **b** 31–40 h **c** 38.4 h
d 0.23
3a

3–3.1	3.1–3.2	3.2–3.3	3.3–3.4
1	2	4	8

3.4–3.5	3.5–3.6	3.6–3.7	3.7–3.8	3.8–3.9
9	1	3	1	0

b mean 3.39, mode 3.45 **d** (i) $\frac{5}{29}$ (ii) 172 cars

PAGE 66   EXERCISE 3F

1 35.2 years **2** 5.46 **3b** 8.42%

PAGE 68   EXERCISE 4F

1a (0, 2), (0, 4), (1, 3), (1, 4), (1, 5), (2, 4), (2, 5), (3, 5),
(3, 6), (3, 7), (4, 5), (4, 6), (4, 8), (5, 5), (5, 6), (6, 7), (6, 8),
(6, 9), (7, 8), (7, 10), (8, 9), (8, 10), (9, 9), (9, 10), (10, 10)
b Mean (4.6, 6.6) **c** (i) (2.2, 4.9) (ii) (7.2, 8.4)
2 Best-fitting line passes through:
a (1.7, 6.2) (3.9, 7.6) (6.1, 8.9)
b (2, 5.8)   (4.5, 4)   (6.8, 2.3)
When $x = 3$ 5   7;
    a $y = 7$ 8 9.5
    b $y = 5$ 3.5   2

14 KINDS OF QUADRILATERAL

PAGE 69   EXERCISE 1F

1a (i) 40 cm, 1 rod; 72 cm, 1 rod; 50 cm, 2 rods;
30 cm, 2 rods; 78 cm, 2 rods (ii) Four 3-way joints;
one 4-way joint **c** 3360 cm²
2a

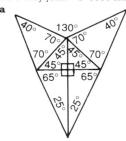

b A V-kite. Diagonal AC is a line of symmetry.
3a (2, 5) **b** (0, 0), (−5, 2), (−5, 5), (−2, 5),
c (0, 0), (5, −2), (5, −5), (2, −5); (0, 0), (−5, −2),
(−5, −5), (−2, −5)

PAGE 69   EXERCISE 2F

1

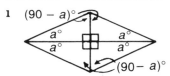

2a 40° and 140° **3** 1.6 m, 1.2 m

PAGE 71   EXERCISE 4F

1b (i) (0, 0), (3, 0), (6, 0), ... (3n−3, 0) where
      n = 1, 2, 3, . . .
   (ii) (1, 2), (4, 2), (7, 2), ... (3n−2, 2) where
      n = 1, 2, 3, . . .
   (iii) (2, 4), (5, 4), (8, 4), ... (3n−1, 4) where
      n = 1, 2, 3, . . .
c No **d** Move one across and two up, etc, from
(3n−3, 0) **e** (i) Yes (ii) Yes (iii) No (iv) Yes
2a (2, 1), (5, 1), (8, 1), (3, 3), (6, 3) **b** From each
flower, move two across and one up.
3a $(2\frac{1}{2}, 1\frac{1}{2})$ **b** (i) (0, 0), (5, 3) (ii) (0, 1), (5, 2)
(iii) (1, 1), (4, 2) and others **4** The points of
intersection of the diagonals of the parallelograms
are equidistant from the kerb.

PAGE 72   EXERCISE 5F

1 ABFG, BCDE; ABEG, BCDF
2b B(3, 2), C(5, 0), D(3, −2), E(−3, −2), F(−5, 0)
3a 45° **b** 23 cm **4a** 68 cm **b** 252 cm²

5a A trapezium
b
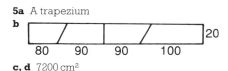

80 90 90 100 20

c, d $7200\,cm^2$

PAGE 73   EXERCISE 6F

1a AD∥BC, or AB = DC   **b** rectangle, parallelogram, square, rhombus, trapezium   **c** all the angles are 75° or 105°   **2a** A square 40 cm by 40 cm, a rectangle 30 cm by 40 cm, a rectangle 50 cm by 40 cm and three right-angled triangles 30 cm by 40 cm by 50 cm   **b** $6600\,cm^2$ **3a** Quadrilateral   **b** trapezium   **c** parallelogram   **d** rectangle   **e** rhombus   **f** square

15 SOME SPECIAL NUMBERS

PAGE 75   EXERCISE 1F

1a 5^3 **b** 2^7 **c** same   **d** 10^1 **e** 4^4 **2a** 64
b 10000   **c** 32   **d** 20   **e** 5   **f** 3   **3a** 4   **b** 1   **c** 2
d 3   **e** 5   **4a** (i) 2^7 (ii) 3^6 (iii) 5^6 (iv) 6^6 (v) 10^8
b add the indices   **c** 2^{a+b} **5a** (i) 3^3 (ii) 4   (iii) 6^3
(iv) 10^4 (v) 2^9 **b** subtract the indices   **c** 2^{a-b}
6a 2^0 **b** $2^5 \div 2^5 = 1 = 2^0$ **c** (i) 1   (ii) 1   (iii) 1

PAGE 76   EXERCISE 2F

1a 576   **b** 19   **c** 2304   **d** 33
2a 19.0   **b** 566   **c** 8.37   **d** 26.5   **3a** 961   **b** 99856
4a (i) 9 m/s   (ii) 12.2 m/s   **b** (i) 19.6 m   (ii) 38.0 m
5a (i) 169   (ii) 13   **b** (i) 821   (ii) 28.7
6a 8.879   **b** 10.289 (positive solution)   **7** 7.07 cm

PAGE 76   EXERCISE 3F

1a Yes   **b** yes   **c** no   **d** no   **e** yes   **f** yes   **2b, e**
3a 8, 16, 24, 32, 40, 48; 12, 24, 36, 48; 24
b 6, 12, 18, 24, 30, 36, 42, 48; 8, 16, 24, 32, 40, 48; 24
c 3, 6, 9, 12, 15, 18, 21, 24, 27, 30, 33, 36;
6, 12, 18, 24, 30, 36; 9, 18, 27, 36; 18   **4a** 40   **b** 60
5a 60 min   **b** 75 min   **c** 180 min   **d** 300 min
6a No   **b** yes

PAGE 78   EXERCISE 4F

1 1, 2, 4, 7, 14, 28   **2** 1, 2, 3, 4, 6, 9, 12, 18, 36
3 1, 2, 4, 5, 8, 10, 20, 40
4 1, 2, 3, 4, 5, 6, 10, 12, 15, 20, 30, 60
5 1, 2, 4, 8, 16, 32, 64
6 1, 2, 3, 4, 5, 6, 8, 10, 12, 15, 20, 24, 30, 40, 60, 120
7a 1, 2, 3, 4, 6, 12; 1, 2, 3, 6, 9, 18   **b** 1, 2, 3, 6   **c** 6
8a 1, 2, 4, 7, 14, 28; 1, 2, 3, 6, 7, 14, 21, 42
b 1, 2, 7, 14   **c** 14

9a 1, 2, 3, 4, 6, 8, 12, 24; 1, 2, 3, 4, 6, 9, 12, 18, 36
b 1, 2, 3, 4, 6, 12   **c** 12
10 20   **11** 8   **12** 12   **13** 18   **14** 25   **15** 16   **16** 30
17 15   **18a** $\frac{4}{5}$ **b** $\frac{3}{4}$ **c** $\frac{7}{10}$ **d** $\frac{3}{8}$ **e** $\frac{13}{20}$ **f** $\frac{5}{24}$

PAGE 78   EXERCISE 5F

1 **d, e, f, g, i, j**   **2a** $14^2 + 7$ **b** $11^2 - 2$ **c** $2^9 - 1$
3 Gives prime numbers except for
$n = 6, 11, 13, 16, 17$ **4a** 5, 17, 37, 101, 197, 257, 401
b $2n^2 - 1$ **5** 9973

PAGE 79   EXERCISE 6F

1 $2 \times 2 \times 2 \times 3$ **2** $2 \times 3 \times 5$ **3** $2 \times 2 \times 2 \times 5$
4 $2 \times 3 \times 11$ **5** $2 \times 5 \times 7$ **6** $3 \times 3 \times 3 \times 3$ **7** $2 \times 2 \times 23$
8 5×19 **9** $2 \times 2 \times 2 \times 3 \times 5$ **10** $2 \times 2 \times 2 \times 5 \times 5$
11 $2 \times 2 \times 2 \times 5 = 40$ **12** $2 \times 2 \times 3 \times 5 = 60$
13 $2 \times 2 \times 3 \times 3 \times 5 = 180$ **14** $2 \times 2 \times 2 \times 2 \times 2 \times 3 = 96$
15 $2 \times 2 \times 5 \times 7 = 140$ **16** 2×3^2 **17** $2^4 \times 3$
18 $2^3 \times 3 \times 5$ **19** $2^4 \times 3^2$ **20** 2^{10} **21** $3^2 \times 5^2$
22 $2^2 \times 3^4$ **23** $2^2 \times 5^2 \times 7^2$ **24** $2^2 \times 5^5$ **25** $2^3 \times 7^3$.

16 FORMULAE AND SEQUENCES

PAGE 80   EXERCISE 1F

1a 44   **b** 38   **c** $N = 50 - x$ **d** (i) $N = 90 - x$
(ii) $N = C - x$ **2a** 3 litres   **b** 11 litres   **c** 17 litres
d (i) $N = \frac{d}{k}$ (ii) $R = S - \frac{d}{k}$
3a 24 000   **b** 25 200   **c** (i) $N = WLP$
(ii) $X = BP, Y = BPL, Z = BPLW$
4a $29\,cm^2$ **b** $52\,cm^2$ **c** $A = LB - n$
d (i) $A = LB - 4n$ (ii) $A = LB - nx^2$
5a $M = \frac{3F}{10}, M = 1.5$ **b** $M = \frac{5K}{8}, M = 20$
c $C = (F - 32) \times \frac{5}{9}; C = 100$
6a $T = 3x + 2y$ **b** $x = \frac{U}{3}$ **c** $x = \frac{(V - 2y)}{3}$
7a (i) $d = y - hx$ (ii) $d = y - \frac{mx}{60}$
b (i) $d = y - h(x + 2)$ (ii) $d = y - \frac{m(x + 2)}{60}$.

PAGE 81   EXERCISE 2F

1a $P = 2a + 2b$ **b** $P = 6u + 6v$ **c** $P = 10c$
2a $P = 10x, 10x, 18x, 22x$
b $P = 2a + 2c, 2b + 2c, 2a + 2b + 2d, 2a + 2b + 2c + 2d$
3 $P = 2rs + 2st$
4a $A = 2a - 1$ **b** $A = xy + yz$ **c** $A = 6xy$

5a $A = 6x^2, 6x^2, 18x^2, 30x^2$
b $A = ac, bc, d(a+b), (a+b)(c+d)$
6a $L = 24y$ **b** $A = 22y^2$ **c** $V = 6y^3$
7 $V = xyz - xyd$ or $V = xy(z-d)$

PAGE 82 EXERCISE 3F

1a Add 2 to the number; A22, A24, A26 **b** Add $\frac{1}{16}$;
$\frac{11}{16}, \frac{3}{4}, \frac{13}{16}$ **c** Add $\frac{1}{16}, \frac{1}{2}, \frac{9}{16}, \frac{5}{8}$
d Differences are 0.09, 0.08, 0.07, ... ;
0.94, 0.99, 1.03 **e** Add 3; 81, 84, 87
2a 13, 21, 34; 89 **b** 17, 28, 45, 73; 191
c 2, 5; 50, 81; 212, 343 **d** 1, 3, 4; 29, 47; 123, 199
e 4, 5; 14; 60; 157, 254
3b A: Differences are 1, 2, 3, 4, 5, 6, 7
   B: Double each term
   C: Differences are 2, 3, 4, 5, 6
   D: Square numbers ($1 \times 1, 2 \times 2, 3 \times 3, ...$)
   E: Differences are $-20, -19, -18, -17, -16, -15$
   F: Differences are $-5^2, -4^2, -3^2, -2^2, -1^2$.
4a $\frac{1}{4}, \frac{1}{2}, 1; 4, 8, 16, ...$ **b** $-14, 9, -5, 4; 5, 7, ...$
c 0, 1, 2; 26, 677, ... **d** 42, 20, 4, 16, 37, 58, 89, 145,
42, ... they repeat **e** 34, 17, 52, 26, 13, 40, 20, 10, 5,
16, 8, 4, 2, 1, 4, 2, 1, ... this also repeats.

Page 83 Challenge

A Add the digit sum; for example, for 23, add $2 + 3$ to
  get 28.
B Divide number by 10, ignoring remainders; add
  the result to get the next number.
C Double the prime numbers 2, 3, 5, 7, 11, ...
D Square the middle digit, then add that to get the
  next number.

PAGE 83 EXERCISE 4F

1a 49th **b** 33rd **c** 59th **d** 117th
2a 1   5 **b** 7   32 **3a** 3   5 **b** 5   38
    2   7   8   37   4   8   4   31
    3   9   9   42   5   11   3   24
    4   11   10   47   6   14   2   17
                           7   17   1   10

PAGE 85 EXERCISE 5F

1a (i) 4 (ii) 12 **b** 4, 12 missing **c** 112;

```
4    12    24    40    60    84    112
  8    12    16    20    24    28
    4    4    4    4    4
```
2a 5 **b** 5 missing
c 495

```
0   1   5   15   35   70   126   210   330   495
  1   4   10   20   35   56   84   120   165
    3   6   10   15   21   28   36   45
      3   4   5   6   7   8   9
        1   1   1   1   1   1
```

17 PROBABILITY

PAGE 86 EXERCISE 1F

1a (i) $\frac{1}{3}$ (ii) $\frac{2}{3}$ **b**
2a 16 **b** 20
3
4a **b** 200
5
6

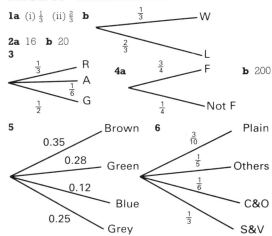

PAGE 87 EXERCISE 2F

1

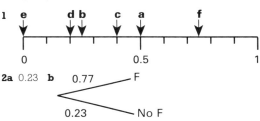

2a 0.23 **b** 0.77
3a (i) 0.00125 (ii) 0.0125 **b** 0.9875
4a 20% **b**
5

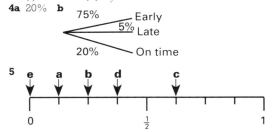

PAGE 87 EXERCISE 3F

Methods: **1** Past data **2** Counting **3** Experiment
4 Experiment **5** Counting **6** Survey **7** Past data
8 Survey

PAGE 88 EXERCISE 4F

1a 143 **b** 83 **c** 3 **d** 1 **2a** 10 to 30 **b** 5 **3** 12
4a 9000 **b** 90 000–100 000 **c** 9000 **5** About £220.